SHOULDERS TO FREEDOM

A Cambodian Diaspora Memoir

MAI BUNLA

ISBN-10: 061576343X

EAN-13: 9780615763439

Library of Congress Control Number: 2013906800

CreateSpace Independent Publishing Platform,
North Charleston, SC

For my family, the Nyaw People,
and
In the memory of Ai Sang Thout,
mom, and dad.

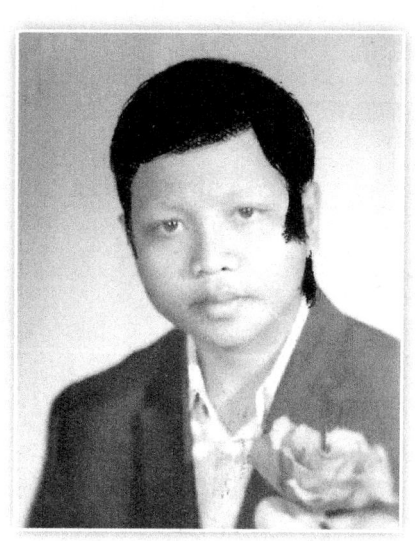

<u>សិវិៃតត្រេសង្ខេបរបស់ប្រុស</u>

នាង ខ្ញុំ ឈ្មោះ ប៊ុនឡូវ វាៃ ភូមិៃ ថ្មៃ ស់ នៅ
កាហ្សង់ អាមេរិក ។ ក្បួម ពំ ក្នុងៃ នេ ការ សង់ គ្រួ ការ ឈ្មោះ ប៊ុនឡូ ៣៖
ដែរ ក្តាន់ បិត ក្តូ នៅ ឆ្នាំ ១៩៧៥ អាយុ ់ អាយុ ១៦ ឆ្នៃ
ក្លាៃ កម្ម ើ សិ៩ ឃ្មាៃ ើ (ស្លៀត អាព្យ) ទង្វ ្រ់ ់ ់ ើ្រ់
(លាង ស់ ិៃ៍ វៃ្ញ ់ ្ញ ចៃ់ ផ្ញៃ ់ ែៃ៍ ្ញ ណេ បុភ្ញៃ ់ មាន ់ ។

ឪ ពាត ឈ្មោះ ប៊ុនឡូវ ប៊ិតស្ញៃ (ស្លៀ), មុយ ឈ្មោះ
ប៊ិនឡូ ័ ១ៃ (ស្ញៃ) ក្នុង ្ញៃ ួ យ ឈ្មោះ ប៊ិនឡូ លាត
(់ ៃ្ន) ក្នុង ្រ ័ ៃ់ ់ ្ញ ើ ឈ្មោះ ប៊ិនឡូ អាត (់ ្រ ្រ់),
ក្នុង ្រ ័ ្ញ ឈ្មោះ ប៊ិនឡូ ព្រៃ (់ ្រ ្រ់), ក្នុង ់ ប្រ ្ញ
ឈ្មោះ ប៊ិនឡូ ់ ្ញ (់ ្រ ្រ់) , ក្នុង ់ ្រ្រ ឈ្មោះ ប៊ិនឡូ វៃ
(្រ ្រ់) ។

ើ ្រៃ ្ញ ្ញ ្ន ។ ្ញ ្ន ់ ឈ្មោះ ប៊ិនឡូ ៣អៃ ់ ៖
ក្ញ ់ ្ញ ់ ់ ្ញ ់ ។ ្ញ ្ញ ្ញ ្ញ ្ញ ើ ៃ ៖ ឈ្មោះ
ប៊ិនឡូ វៃ ។

This is the original and the only photo I have of my brother who was captured by the Khmer Rouge in 1975. This picture was taken sometime in 1974 after his novice training. The 1970s hairstyle was sketched in by a studio artist at my bother's requested. I used this photo and this Cambodian text as this book's cover because I am still searching for any information about him. This same information was announced on a Cambodian radio station, advertised in a Cambodian newspaper called Khmer Surlang, archived in the Documentary Center of Cambodia (DC-CAM), and written about in the Phnom Penh Post. A summary of this translation includes the following: *his name, when and where the Khmer Rouge took him, and all the family names. If you know any information about this man, please contact the author.*

Table of Contents

Acknowledgments

I would like to express my sincere thanks to the many people who saw me through this book; to all those who provided me support, talked things over, read, wrote, offered comments, allowed me to quote their names, and assisted in the editing, proofreading and designing. There are too many names to mention, but you know who you are.

I want to thank my editor, Melissa Grossman, for her contributions. Thank you for catching mistakes and suggesting additions that I would have otherwise not thought of. I want to also thank Jen Harris who designed the book cover and worked with me to get the message across.

To my family, words can never express how much I love you and appreciate you. You all have impacted my life in such a good way and I thank you. To my sisters, Let and Lai, you are my rocks. To my daughter, Sophie Kanjana Rosenstock, thank you for being patient throughout this process. You are my life and my inspiration. Without you this book would not exist.

Introduction

I wrote this memoir for two reasons: the desire to keep the memory of my oldest brother alive and the longing to know better the people and the place I come from, the Nyaw.

According to oral tradition, the Nyaw came to Cambodia by way of Laos, from north of Vientiane. There are no written documents about or by the Nyaw people, only history passed by word of mouth. I grew up confused and unsure about where my family originated and ashamed that I didn't know such basic things. It made me feel like I didn't belong anywhere.

My parents and grandparents were born in Cambodia, but they were originally from the Xieng Khuang province in Laos and of a Lao ethnic minority, the Nyaw. The Nyaw people, like the majority of Lao people, left their lands during the nineteenth century when Thailand defeated Laos, and the Thai depopulation of Laos began. Since then, Nyaw people have scattered throughout Laos, Thailand, and Cambodia. Today in the regions of Laos and Thailand, the Nyaw population is estimated to be about twenty thousand, if not more. In the Sisophon province in Banteay Meanchey, Cambodia and Allanyaprethet, Thailand there are many Nyaw villages and currently there are approximately 5,000 Nyaw families living there. In the West, approximately fifteen hundred families live in Long Beach, California, the largest concentration of Nyaw in the United States. About fifty families are in Northern California and one thousand are in France, Australia, Canada, and Switzerland. A few years ago, I read an article about how the Japanese government was worried about a decrease in population, and I could not help but think about how the Nyaw people hovered at the brink of extinction.

Our language is a mixture of Thai and Lao but with a slight accent between the two. Most of us grew up speaking Nyaw, Thai, Cambodian, and Lao, but today, like its population, the Nyaw language barely exists. This decline began when the language was supplanted by the more mainstream Lao during the Thai depopulation. Since Nyaw wasn't a recognized language, it wasn't widely used. Over time each generation adapted to the mainstream language of where they lived and forgot their native language altogether. Before the Khmer Rouge takeover the Nyaw people in the Sisophon province continued to speak Nyaw but also Thai, Cambodian, and Lao. During the time of the Khmer Rouge, it was dangerous to speak anything but Cambodian. Speaking other languages made you and your entire family a target of suspicion, and subject to execution, disappearance, or death by starvation. Because of this, the Nyaw dared not speak their language for a long time. Those still living in Sisophon province learned to speak Cambodian perfectly.

Those of us who fled the atrocities of the Khmer Rouge and escaped to the West are the last but significant reason why the Nyaw language is spoken less and less. We've had to overcome the challenges of new cultures, languages, and habits, and we've busied ourselves with integrating into our new communities. Keeping our native language alive has been the least of our worries. This is sad but true.

Even before the Khmer Rouge regime left its mark on the Nyaw, in 1907 the French drew a map for their now former colony that annexed a chunk of the Battambang territory of Thailand to Cambodia had an impact as well. In their eyes they were restoring land to Cambodia that Thailand had seized during the later half of the 18th century. Prior to 1907, my village, Ban Doug Alaan, was part of Thailand, but after the annexation it became Cambodia. The redrawing of the territorial map divided the Nyaw. Half of us were pronounced to be citizens of Cambodia, and the other half were pronounced to be Thai.

Since childhood I have struggled with identity. To this day, Cambodian people refer to me as "Leo Khmer" or "Lao Cambodian," as if to imply that I am Lao first and Cambodian second. Technically, this is correct, but the effect is that I feel Cambodian people don't accept me as one of them. Likewise, Laotian people refer to me as "Khmen Lao" or "Cambodian Lao," and so it seems that the Lao people deny me as one of them too, despite coming from an indigent Laotian tribe. To both the Cambodians and the Lao, I am an outsider, and the Nyaw are outsiders. A feeling of not being accepted was and is always a bad thing to experience, whether as a child or as an adult. I grew up always wondering where I belonged.

It may be cliché, but becoming a mother compelled me to tell my story, compelled me to sort through and face memories and stories I avoided growing up. By doing so, I hope that my daughter, nieces, and nephews never have to go through life wondering, as I did, who they are and about the family history behind them.

However, what truly inspired and pushed me to put these memories into a book, even more than a quest for an understanding of my own identity, was the memory of my oldest brother, Ai Sang Thout. He was one of the nearly two million Cambodians who fell victim to the Khmer Rouge during its rule from 1975 to 1980. When the Khmer took him away in the summer of 1975, I was about seven years old. No one heard from him again. Unable to understand what had happened, I began to fear that the Khmer Rouge would come again and again and take away everyone I loved, one by one, until I was the only one left. I lived with this fear for a long time.

Besides losing my oldest brother, like most other Cambodians, we also lost many members of our extended family while the Khmer Rouge was in power. Aunts, uncles, and cousins died from starvation, forced labor, diseases, and outright murder. This certainly challenged my family's endurance, but it was Ai Sang Thout's disappearance that affected me the most.

For a number of years, I truly believed in my heart that he was alive, perhaps working as forced labor for the Khmer Rouge. The saddest part for me was that I also believed he spent many nights praying to be reunited with us, his family.

To this day, there is some part of me that refuses to believe that he is no longer in this world. I want my fantasies about our reunion to come true, even though my gut tells me they won't. It's a hard fact I've struggled to accept.

There is one last reason why I have put this memoir into print, and it is based on a small wish of great hope. One day I hope to know the truth about what happened to Ai Sang Thout after he was taken from us. Someone out in the larger world, someone who knew of him or his fate, might read this memoir. If so, this memoir will in a way reunite me with my brother or at least provide me with some answers. I pray that this is not the end of our story, that this memoir will someday require an update or a sequel.

PART I
WHAT WAS

Ban Doug Alaan

While Neil Armstrong took his first step on the moon in 1969, I took my first breath in the tiny village of Ban Doug Alaan in Cambodia's Sisophon province. That was the name of the village in Nyaw, although in Cambodian it was called Phnom Dough Alaan. I was the youngest of five children born into a family of rice farmers. Our village consisted of only about twenty families, most of whom were my relatives.

Like most Cambodian villages, Ban Doug Alaan was surrounded by rice paddies. Most houses were made of bamboo and straw, with a thatched roof. Fruit trees bordered the village on all sides—mango, guava, banana, papaya, and tamarind. Chickens and pigs roamed the streets. Every animal knew which family they belonged to without tags stapled into their wings or ears. Cows and bulls grazed freely in the field. Children ran loose, nearly naked, as if they had no cares in the world. Guard dogs kept an eye out for strangers, and grannies sat on their porches watching the day go by, calmly chewing betel nuts.

We didn't have electricity, running water, a market, or cars. Our village had one tiny shop that carried medicines of questionable quality from Thailand that we resorted to using only when the village healer had exhausted all of his or her healing powers or when the monk's mantra or holy water didn't work. Since there were no cars, people walked everywhere, and if we needed to go somewhere beyond walking distance—to visit the Angkor Wat for example—we flagged down a ride of some sort on the main road.

By village standards, if you owned a bicycle or a motorbike, you were rich; if you owned a wagon and a few cows, you were middle class; and if you had none of these things you were poor. Still no one went hungry because we shared the vegetables we grew in our gardens, the fish we caught in the river, and the animals we slaughtered. A neighbor might swap some chicken for a cut of pork. We even shared the turtles, birds, wild boars, snakes, forest rats, and edible bugs that the men brought back from their hunt. You name it, we ate it. That was the way it was in my village back then. Compared to the way things changed later on, I didn't have much, yet I had everything.

To one side of our house there was a path lined with palm trees that led to an aunt's house. Banana trees grew on the opposite side of our house next to the kitchen and the wooden steps that led to the house. This was a favorite place for our pig and her piglets to roam. I recall sitting on the steps one day, not long before the Khmer Rouge took over, playing with my parents' and siblings' flip-flops, trying to figure out which one went on which foot. No matter how hard I tried, I couldn't match left foot to left flip-flop or right foot to right flip-flop. I spent an hour staring at the family shoes but would sometimes glance up at the rows and rows of banana trees. The pig and her piglets oinked around me several times, but I paid them no mind. In the end, I never figured out which shoe belonged to which foot, but by the end of the hour, I had taken a mental snapshot of our house, a picture I've never forgotten.

My life in the village was carefree, at least until I was about seven. Even as a toddler it was safe for me to roam since most of the people around were my relatives. There was no shortage of cousins and friends. Being the youngest I was a bit overprotected by my family, especially by my mother and oldest brother, Ai Sang Thout. Like my mother, I wasn't much of a talker. I was a shy kid who liked to shadow other people and let them do all the talking for me. Except for the time I tried to voice my opinion in protest when my father shaved off my hair to get rid of the lice.

* * *

My mother grew up in Ban Doug Alaan. She received most of life's lessons there, married there, and gave birth to seven children. (Five lived, and two died right after birth.) Born in 1934, Mom was the middle child among five girls and no boys. The family was poor, not owning even a wagon or any cows. Her family worked for other people, mainly in the fields. The only land they owned was the small plot on which their little thatched roof hut stood and a small garden plot filled with all kinds of fruit trees. As her sisters came of age, they married villagers from nearby. These men were like a second set of fathers to me. Her parents approved of these arrangements because it ensured that the villagers could intervene if the couples became embroiled in a marital dispute, which did happen from time to time.

My mother never spoke about her youth, so I don't know what she was like as a young girl. Other people might go on and on about their childhood, but my mother would only say, "I was just a simple village girl. All I knew was the village way of life: when it was time to sleep, I slept; when it was time to eat, I ate; and when it was time to work, I worked. That was all."

A shy person of few words, my mother was very modest in everything she did. Since there are no photos of her as a young girl, I can only imagine what she looked like and can only assume she was pretty. It must have been so because my father courted her, and he was a handsome young man.

Unlike her sisters, my mother married into a family that wasn't as familiar to her own family. Although Dad was half Nyaw (his mother was Nyaw, and his father was Phuan, another ethnic Laotian tribe from

5

the same area as the Nyaw people) Mom's family had reservations about him. He came from a family of landowners, and they didn't trust them.

The way my parents met sounds like a typical story for Nyaw people back in those days. The first time Dad noticed Mom was when his family moved to her village. Family names mattered, but in their village my mother's family name had little value. My father must have known this, but it didn't stop him from pursuing her. I think Dad was a modern thinker, which is why, when he saw her and liked her, he didn't care about her background. I've always liked that about him.

When I asked them who first courted whom, my father replied, "Your mom courted me," with a smirk on his face. My mother, being truly a person of few words, merely rolled her eyes at him. When they married, he was eighteen and she was nineteen.

When I asked how my father's family came to live in Ban Doug Alaan, it is a familiar tale of upheaval and migration.

In 1945 there was an anti-French Khmer nationalist group called the Khmer Issaraks that attempted to expel the French colonial authorities from Cambodia. This movement took place mainly in the Battambang province and it disrupted my father's village since his village was near the conflicted areas. Because of this, he explained, "The Thai people looted the whole village. Many people were hurt and some were killed. The village was no longer safe, and there was nothing they could do because they were nobodies. So we moved," he lamented, shaking his head.

Having been in the business of owning land in their old village, my grandfather looked for the same opportunity in their new one. Luckily, there was a large piece of land about a half mile away that no one wanted to claim. It was overgrown with forest, and it had been deemed that nothing would grow there. Being an optimistic person, my grandfather declared ownership of the land. The whole family pitched in to clear it and in no time turned it into a rice farm. It was also a perfect piece of land for farming. Even a river ran through it. That was my grandfather's claim to fame in the village.

When it was safe for my father's family to return to their old village, he was given the rice farm, along with three cows, one buffalo, and a wagon. By then he had married my mother and expressed a wish to remain where he was. With these gifts, my parents began a life together. They built a house situated in the heart of the village, across the street from my maternal grandparents.

It was in this wooden, tin-roofed house on stilts that I was born. Small, it had a living room and a bedroom, and an attached kitchen. The rooms were bare and without furniture, except for one wooden box in the bedroom in which we stored our good formal clothes. I remember there were many nails in the house poles that we used to hang the clothes we wore every day and plastic bags containing miscellaneous items. The ground floor was for storage and a place for gathering. This was where neighbors stopped by any time for a visit, where gossip happened, where I played hide-and-seek with my cousin friends, and where I napped in a hammock during the day.

After I was born, my parents were doing well enough to buy another small rice farm. My father also wanted to open a rice mill in the village, because taking the harvested rice to another village to be hashed was time consuming and wasted money. It would have been a good business, since there was no rice mill in the village, but the Khmer Rouge came into power and everything changed.

Waves of Change

I n Nyaw, "Kaman Dang" means Khmer Rouge or "Red Cambodian." In time that term became for me a synonym for "monster": a huge, hairy, hideous red monster with eyes in the back of its head and gigantic teeth. It hid on the ground floor of our house at night and waited to snatch me and take me away for good. It was the kind of monster that lurked in children's nightmares. Even adults looked over their shoulders at the mention of Kaman Dang, as if something eerie might be creeping toward them from behind.

Before the Khmer Rouge stepped foot in our village, though, a steady stream of Vietnamese passed through. Some of them sought shelter among us for a few days. They came because their village wasn't safe, my mother explained in Nyaw, the language we spoke at home at the time.

For a few months, the Vietnamese families came and went. They traded their gold for food and shelter, and stayed for a while before moving on. It was after the Vietnamese left that I began to see Khmer Rouge soldiers in our village. Sometimes they stopped for a lunch break, but most often they were only passing through. I was seven years old, but the sight of the Khmer Rouge, even with their smiling faces, made me rush inside the house and remain there until they left.

Decades later, in the comfort of our living room in the States, I asked my father if he spoke with the soldiers and tried to find out why they were there. He chatted with them, he told me, but none of them revealed very much. When I grilled him as to why he didn't probe further, he explained that he didn't want to draw attention.

"We just wanted to be left alone," he said.

"But did you think the Khmer Rouge were bad people or good people?" I pressed.

"In the beginning we weren't sure. Some of us were wary of them, but we agreed to wait and see what would happen. We soon learned that they were killers," he answered.

* * *

Sometime after the Khmer Rouge began to appear regularly, I noticed everyone acting strangely one night. Usually after dinner Dad would wash up and do odd jobs around the house. If he left the house in the evening, normally he would say where he was going and when he would be back. This time, though, he just disappeared after dinner without a word, and Mom acted like nothing was wrong. It was dark out, my father was not home, and I became curious.

"Where's Dad?" I asked my mother.

"At a meeting," she said.

"What sort of meeting?"

"A grown-up meeting, Mai."

"What sort of grown-up meeting, and what do they talk about?"

"Mai, you ask too many questions!" Impatient with me, she got up, straightened her sarong, and left me.

Her reaction confused me. Puzzled as to what I had done to make her leave, I went looking for my sisters, Let and Lai. The house was too quiet. When I found them in the kitchen, they shooed me away before I could say one pestering word. Undeterred, I parked myself away from them yet near enough to eavesdrop, except they were mostly silent. Bored, I went in search of my mother and found her sitting on the edge of the stairs by herself, keeping watch like a guard dog. A shirt that needed mending was in her hands, but her hands were idle. She kept checking the dark road and jumped at the sound of my approach. I settled next to her but didn't say a word for fear that she would walk away again. I watched her watching the dark night. Eventually, I fell asleep on the cool wooden floor next to her.

The next morning I was happy to see Dad back at home, but the relief was short lived when I learned where he had been the night before. Men from our village and our neighboring villages had met to form a plan for us to escape, to leave Cambodia. Dad and Mom gathered all of us and whispered that the Khmer Rouge was killing people. Because of this we might have to leave our home soon. We would go to Thailand, which wasn't too far away.

My father and the other men continued to meet to organize the escape, but in the midst of this early stage, the most unthinkable happened. The village leader announced that by order of the new ruling authority, the Khmer Rouge, families from the cities would be coming to live and work among us. Moreover, Khmer Rouge soldiers would be assigned to live in the village to guide and protect us.

"We knew what this meant," my father explained years later. "The Khmer Rouge soldiers intended to control not protect us. We knew what the consequences would be if we didn't cooperate, so we had no choice but to play along."

To make matters worse for our family, two Khmer Rouge soldiers were assigned to live with us for two weeks. This shocked us all but especially my father. He sensed that the regime knew about the plan to escape, and that the soldiers were assigned to live with us so they could keep an eye on him. Why else were we chosen from a few other families in the village? My father lost sleep dwelling on this question, but there was nothing he could do. To object or question this mandate would have put us at risk. My father forced himself to smile in agreement when the news was given to him, and all the while he feared that the soldiers saw how hard it was for him to do so.

A few days prior to the arrival of the two Khmer Rouge soldiers, my father repeatedly told my sisters and brothers and me the dos and don'ts of how to behave around the soldiers.

We were instructed to do everything we could to stay away from them. We were to stay in pairs and not be alone, to stay busy or pretend to be busy. This way the soldiers would not have an opportunity to brainwash us.

"They are not your friends no matter how friendly they are," my father warned.

By late spring of 1975 the presence of Khmer Rouge could be seen and felt everywhere in the village. There were many changes, and they affected everyone. The Khmer Rouge assigned everyone to a workforce, depending on age and gender. Ai Sang Thout was living and working with boys his age at a nearby area. All the adults worked long hours under Khmer Rouge supervision. The Khmer Rouge monitored the village all hours of the day. The whole area was restricted, and there was no more hunting. My cousins and I were afraid to roam the village like we used to. In order to be a collective society, our home and lands were no longer ours. The Khmer Rouge took everything we owned. My father was awestruck by the news. To make sense of these changes, the villagers were forced to covertly gather whatever information they could. Scared and deeply troubled by the upheaval in their lives, many speculated that the Khmer Rouge knew about our plan to escape to Thailand, leading to the general feeling that our fates were in Buddha's hand.

When the city people arrived, they settled in the few open spaces available in the village. During their first week, they slept on the ground and without a roof over their heads, but by the second week, they had all managed to build some sort of shelter for their families. The regime assigned my father the job of overseeing the newcomers, a role that made him sick to his stomach. Each day he took a group of them to work in the rice fields. My father desperately wanted to stay under the radar of the Khmer Rouge and not associate with them, but this assignment made that impossible. The Khmer Rouge would sometimes ask him for a report on how well the new people were doing. These responsibilities were not of my father's choosing or liking but primarily a decision between life and death. Luckily, though, in the early stage of the war, no one we knew personally was killed. My father made a point to report generally when the Khmer Rouge asked him about a worker.

For me, the only thing that felt normal during the takeover was that I still slept in the same house, sandwiched between Mom and Lai. Other than this, I was given many restrictions. My mother constantly hounded me to not trust people, and I could no longer run loose. I was no longer carefree. I no longer went to my cousins house to play, and there were no more gatherings at my grandmother's because that would be seen as suspicious behavior—we might be passing information or conspiring against the Khmer Rouge regime.

"No matter how young and innocent you are," my father insisted, "you are still being watched."

The two Khmer Rouge soldiers who stayed in our home were married and in their mid-twenties. We did not know if they had kids. They maintained a calm demeanor and the appearance of being trustworthy. They greeted the elders with respect and spoke kindly to the kids. They were always together, and never left each other's side. From what I saw of them, they didn't seem at all mean. I could definitely tell that they were not city people by their manners and manner of speaking. Their uniforms consisted of plain black tops and bottoms that looked like pajamas, and they always wore a red-and-white-checkered *korma*, the Khmer Rouge signature scarf.

For as long as the soldiers stayed with us, Dad assigned Lai and my brother, Ath, chores to be done outside since they were too young to participate in the Khmer Rouge workforce. Lai tended the garden and collected firewood. Ath tried to keep busy doing the same. My father was assigned to work away from home but returned home at the end of the workday. But Ai Sang Thout, who was assigned to a work camp away from home along with the other kids his age, had to live at that work camp but was allowed to come home on weekends. He and some of our male cousins did heavy-duty work, mainly moving dirt to build roads. I spent most of my time staying out of the way yet always within sight of my mother, just as my father had asked.

Let, on the other hand, was not as lucky. Since she did all the cooking for the family, she often bumped into our houseguests. Although the soldiers cooked their own food, they prepared it in our kitchen. The arrangement was that we made our meal first, but sometimes the preparations overlapped. Whenever she could, our mother made a point of assisting Let in the kitchen, but this didn't happen often enough. Her work assignment with other women around the village made it hard for her to be with Let as much as she wanted. One time I caught the Khmer Rouge soldiers talking to Let. I was too far to hear the conversation, but I saw that Let kept nodding. As the soldiers left, they lightly tapped her on the head, a cultural sign that meant, "You're an all right kid."

"I saw the Khmer Rouge talking to Let," I whispered to my father when he returned home from work that day. As soon as the Khmer Rouge soldiers were out of sight, Dad grilled Let about the incident while the rest of us listened.

"What did they say to you?" Dad wanted to know.

"They asked me my name and how old I was. That was all," Let answered.

"You see, they were checking to see if I told the truth about your age," he said. "Had you answered that you were older, they would have put you with other kids to do work outside the house. Do your best to avoid them, all of you."

My father had more encounters with the two Khmer Rouge soldiers than any of us. At home, the soldiers and Dad made small talk about seemingly unimportant issues. I was always too far away to hear their conversations, but it sounded to me like my father mostly just said "yes" to whatever was being discussed. I noticed how Dad habitually greeted the soldiers with a big smile, as if they were his good friends. He seemed genuine and sincere toward them, but it was a calculated gesture on his part. Whenever the soldiers were away from our house to attend one of their meetings, our family would hold our own brief gathering, so my father could reiterate his point that these men were dangerous and not to be trusted.

It was utterly taboo to openly acknowledge the fact that most of the villagers did not support the Khmer Rouge. I often overheard my father and his friends whisper their fears that the Khmer Rouge knew this truth. Nonetheless, and despite all the new faces in the village and the heightened fear, the plan to escape persisted. To deflect any suspicions that the Khmer might have about us, the villagers of Ban Doug Alaan pretended to be grateful for the presence of the Khmer Rouge and for its guidance and protection. To keep the peace, they praised the Khmer Rouge and gave the soldiers whatever they wanted. "They lied with their smiles," my father once told me. To an outsider our village appeared as harmonious as ever. The reality, though, was very different. Although the Khmer Rouge had not done us any harm since the takeover, all the signs of the coming destruction were there. People from the city had been moved to the country, families were separated, and the Khmer Rouge kept tabs about everything and everyone. We lived in an atmosphere of perpetual tension and worry.

The Escape

About a month after the Khmer Rouge takeover, my father received unexpected news. One evening a man from the escape committee arrived while the soldiers were out of sight to say that a date for the escape had been set. Some villagers had learned that the current group of Khmer Rouge soldiers would soon rotate to another village. The rotation presented a window of opportunity for us, because the new soldiers might not be as aware of any families suddenly missing, and no one would be meticulously guarding us while the soldiers were busy shifting posts.

It was a very risky plan, yet it was crucial to leave during this first opportunity. It didn't take much effort to persuade people to agree to it, because no one could dispute the truths unraveling right before their eyes. The details of the plan were carefully plotted, and all the families in our village and the surrounding areas were instructed about what to do and where to meet. I am proud to say that even the "new people" from the city were invited to collaborate with the people of my village. In the end, half of the villagers and half of the new people chose to make the dangerous journey.

The day before the escape my father requested permission from the Khmer Rouge for our family to stay at a hut in the rice field. The permission was granted. Until the Khmer Rouge took over, this hut had belonged to us, and we had used it as a place to overnight during the harvest season when there was so much work and not enough time. The Khmer Rouge didn't know that this hut was close to the escape route we would take the next day.

Although I had known for some time about the possibility of leaving the only place I had ever called home, I hadn't grasped the reality of it. My parents did not tell me that we would be leaving Ban Doug Alaan for Thailand until the evening before and only hours from when we would make our break. The news came as a shock. As a child I was somewhat aware of what was going on but not all of it. I knew that my parents worried a lot, but I hadn't realized the situation was so bad that we would have to actually flee.

My father asked us to be very cooperative the following morning. He said we had to be quiet and get plenty of sleep that night because the next day would involve a long walk. At that my parents went back to their preparations, leaving my brother and sisters and me tongue-tied. I overheard my father tell my mother, "It is now or never."

Later that evening, my mother ventured off by herself to fetch Ai Sang Thout from his work site. No one uttered the word "escape." I can imagine how surprised Ai Sang Thout must have felt when Mom appeared and told him to come with her. He didn't resist, my mother told me, because his cousins also left to be with their families.

That night my anxieties about leaving kept me from a peaceful sleep. The thought of leaving became more and more frightening. So many different worries battled in my head. Who would feed the chickens, the pigs and the dogs? Who would care for our house and pick fruit from our trees? Would I see my cousin friends again? How long would we have to be away? When would we move back? I wanted so much to talk with someone, but since I couldn't, I tossed and turned throughout the night. Every position was equally uncomfortable. Now and again I heard pots banging as my mother prepared dried food and grunting sounds as my father tried to tie our few possession together.

The escape morning approached too fast. At dawn Mom tapped me and whispered in my ear, "It's time, Mai." Everyone got up quietly, and within minutes we were ready.

Because I had dozed off and on throughout the night, I was afraid I would be too tired to walk and become a burden to my family. I remember telling myself, *You better be on your best behavior, Mai! No matter the discomfort, don't fuss.*

As we were about to depart from the emptied hut, I had what I can best describe as an anxiety attack. First I went numb. So I marched in a tiny circle until my body came back to life. Then came the urge to pee, but I suppressed it because I didn't want anyone to have to wait for me. After that, even though it was a warm morning, I became so cold that my teeth chattered and it was hard to breathe, as if I was in an icebox. I was so annoyed at myself for feeling all this. Luckily, the anxieties subsided as soon as we left the hut. As we walked, behind us the hut disappeared into the shadows. All of a sudden, off in the distance, we heard dogs barking as if they were sending us a warning signal to be careful. Dad halted, and so did the rest of us. He stared in the direction of the dogs. Like little soldiers following their commander, we imitated him. It was an eerie feeling to hear dogs barking in the dark and from a direction where we knew no one lived.

I pleaded to myself that this was not a sign the Khmer Rouge was coming for us. Surely that same thought was on my father's mind, because he quickly turned toward our destination and picked up speed. Ai Sang Thout swooped me onto his shoulder. I remember thinking, *But I want to continue to walk, damn it!* I'd made that promise to myself to be good, though, so I didn't put up a fight. Plus I could just imagine Ai Sang Thout dragging me along like a sack of potatoes just so we could keep up with the others.

My father led the way at a fast pace and the rest of us tried to keep up with him like clumsy speed walkers. We moved in total silence, with my mother, Ath, and my sisters in the middle. Ai Sang Thout was the last in line with me glued to his shoulder. We slipped, slid, and tripped over many things and stepped on sharp objects, but no one cried out. Aside from our flip-flops and Ai Sang Thout's heavy breathing, only the sound of the insects humming filled the morning air. It was with great relief when we finally met up with the other escapees—people from our village, from nearby villages, and the new people.

My father's family did not take part in this journey, and they had no idea of what we were undertaking. Dad had not been able to visit with them since the takeover because they lived too far away, and because the Khmer Rouge placed too many restrictions on what we could and could not do.

The relatives who left with us were from my mother's side of the family: my grandmother, four of my aunties and their husbands, and many cousins. My grandfather couldn't walk, so he decided against taking this risky journey. The aunt who stayed behind, Auntie Hien, thought that she could ride out the war with her husband and her two daughters, and care for our grandfather.

As soon as we all reached the meeting point, everyone scrambled to get themselves and their belongings across the river. The other children and I rode on a homemade bamboo raft that was dragged and pushed by the adults who could swim. It was here that I first glimpsed how my sister, Lai, who was only about nine years old at the time, so naturally took charge. She wasn't one to wait around to be told what to do. Lai said to Dad, "Let's do this," and without hesitation she helped place our belongings onto the raft and helped the adults push the raft until her feet no longer touched the dirt.

We were in a dangerous zone, not too far off the main road. Tensions were high because soon the Khmer Rouge would also be on the road to their new village. The men on the other side of the river waved impatiently, urging us to move faster. Their eyes darted back and forth between the road, the river, and the dense forest. Everyone who had already made it across held on tight to their belongings, prepared to run for their lives. We moved quickly, yet every minute seemed like an eternity. Finally, after our entire group had crossed the river, we disappeared into the dense forest and began our exodus to Thailand.

During the first hours of the march no one said a word. Animals and insects ran for cover as we invaded their territory. Except for the cracking of tree branches made by the men at the front to clear a path, and the crackling of dry leaves underfoot, the forest was silent.

My father kept an eye on everyone, making sure we didn't stray. In addition to the belongings he carried in his arms, Let and Lai were carried by turns on his back. My mother carried our cooking utensils and food. Ath carried a pair of shoes. Ai Sang Thout was responsible for me. With heavy hearts, we trudged onward.

I don't recall a lot about the trip, but I clearly remember everything that happened between Ai Sang Thout and me, since from Cambodia all the way to Thailand he carried me on his shoulders. At times I dozed off. Slouched over, I was a much more difficult bundle for him to manage.

"Wake up and sit up straight!" he commanded me several times. I would rouse myself only to drift off again seconds later

"I will make you walk if you don't sit up!" he threatened.

I was so tired that although I replied, "OK," almost immediately I would fall asleep again.

Fed up, Ai Sang Thout lowered me to the ground and motioned for me to walk. I obeyed without complaint, though it was hard to navigate the path in near darkness. I stumbled and softly cried "ouch!" a few times. Ai Sang Thout held on to my hand and kept me from falling over. Five minutes later he dropped to his knees and said, "Come on," pulling me gently toward him. Once again I climbed onto his back.

"I could still walk if you want me to," I whispered in his ear, and to this he said, "That's all right. I'll take care of you. Go to sleep now." For the rest of the trip, I drifted in and out of sleep, waking now and again to slap away the tree branches that scratched my arms and legs or when the tickling of the leaves annoyed me.

Several times I felt a sharp pain on my lower back. "Brother, something is hurting my back," I told Ai Sang Thout. When he turned around to inspect, we were looking at a woman coming directly at us with a bamboo carrying stick, the kind farmers use to carry watering cans or balance heavy loads. She was half asleep and didn't realize that she had jabbed me with the sharp ends of her stick. Ai Sang Thout moved out of her way to avoid further injury.

As the sun began to rise, most of the people were already exhausted. The fast pace set at the beginning of the journey had slowed down dramatically. We moved like drunk people. My mother held onto Ath's hand so in his fatigue he didn't get lost. The one time she let go he crashed into a bush, yet still clinging to his pair of shoes. These were not just any shoes, you see. They were tennis shoes with laces, a rarity for villagers who only wore flip-flops. These shoes were so special to Ath that he chose to carry rather than wear them as we made our way through the forest. It took the combined strength of my parents, everything they had, to pull him upright from the bush. Disoriented, as if he had just woken from a deep sleep, Ath shook his head, still clinging to those damn shoes.

Thirty exhausted families plodding through a forest inevitably make some noise. People moaned out of pure tiredness; children cried because they didn't want to move another inch. One of the most disturbing sights I saw were two young children on the side of the road crying for their parents. It made me hold on to Ai Sang Thout extra tight.

"Mom, Dad, where are you?" they cried aloud in Cambodian. Their wails turned only a few heads. Most people hurried away from them, afraid the Khmer Rouge might hear the racket. As we approached, one man begged the children to not make too much noise.

I will always remember the sight of them, a boy and a girl. The girl was about my age, and the boy appeared to be a year or so older. They clung to each other as they leaned against a rock for support. They looked like children who had been evacuated from the city and joined our group. Dad approached them. Our whole family followed him reluctantly.

My father dropped to his knees and asked the children when they had last seen their parents.

"We don't know," the boy answered through tears.

"You will find them later, but for now you and your sister must continue with the rest of us," Dad told them.

"We can't walk because we are sick. Our parents were also sick when we last saw them," the boy said.

It wasn't clear if their father had been part of our group. My father suspected that only their mother had attempted the journey, but being too ill had fallen behind and got lost. My father did the only thing he knew how to do, and that was a Buddhist healing ritual for the children. He tossed a tiny piece of areca nut into his mouth and chewed on it while chanting a mantra. Then Dad took a deep breath and blew on the children's heads, spraying bits of the nut and saliva. Then with three more deep breaths, he blew only cool air, once, twice, and a third time. I had seen my father do this ritual a million times and had received my share of his healing powers. No matter the illness or discomfort, he would give me a dose of his medicine.

After the ritual we paced in circles, waiting for it to work its magic on the children. On my father's face we could all see his struggle with this difficult situation and the decision about what to do next. He half-smiled as he looked over to my mother who was, by this time, getting impatient as she watched the crowd passing us by.

"Can we take them with us?" Dad quietly asked her.

Mom went pale. She reasoned with my father that our hands were already full without having to care for sick children. Besides, there was no guarantee that we would even make it out of this forest alive.

"We have to go. The others have passed us," my mother said.

My father reluctantly took Let and Lai by the hand and forced himself onward, and we followed him. Behind us was the most sorrowful sight, two frightened souls holding on to each other. To this day, we have no idea what became of the children.

* * *

We had been out of the forest and on open road for a good two hours when we stopped for our first rest. The group leader had brought us to the main road once we reached what was presumed to be a safer area.

Mom handed each of us a ball of sticky rice and a stick of beef jerky for our breakfast. After we ate, almost everyone sank into a deep sleep. A few children stayed awake, looking bored. Lai and I were among them. Lai sat on top of a small pile of rocks by herself. I sat beside Ai Sang Thout, since he never allowed me to leave his side. Suddenly we heard a man shout from afar. At first we couldn't make out what he said, but soon enough we heard the warning clearly.

"Run! The Khmer Rouge is coming. Run and hide!" the voice commanded. Everyone awoke, startled by the alarm, and dispersed in chaos into the jungle.

Ai Sang Thout snatched me by the waist and headed to a nearby bush. He ran right into it, holding me in front of him. I closed my eyes at the point of impact. Ai Sang Thout persisted, pushing, and shoving at the vines so hard that I thought the vines might cut me in half. I bit my lips to stop myself from crying out, but in my head I shouted for him to stop. Finally the vines gave way, and we tumbled forward. I closed my eyes and braced myself, certain whatever happened next would be painful. We landed with a hard thump. My face smashed into leaves and branches, but to my surprise (and relief) I wasn't hurt. Ai Sang Thout had used one hand to stop his weight from flattening me. He half covered me with his body, and we kept still, wrapped in vines and all sorts of shrubbery that camouflaged us from the enemy.

I looked at him as if to ask a question, but he silently gestured for me to shush and remain still. We didn't dare move any part of our bodies and only blinked our eyes to communicate. I couldn't see nor hear anyone else. I heard only our thumping heartbeats.

Don't you dare move, Mai, I repeated to myself, at the same time musing how nice the earth smelled and how special it was to be protected. These oddly pleasant thoughts were disrupted by a friendly call to come out from hiding.

When we emerged, I heard Dad cry, "*Oy! Lerm E-Lai.* (Damn it! We forgot about Lai.)" As it turned out, she was still sitting on the pile of rocks, the only person left in the open road. In the midst of chaos, everyone had forgotten about her. Dad rushed over to her with a "forgive me?" smile on his face. There was no time, though, to find out if Lai felt abandoned or to comfort her for we were on the move again. A trooper, Lai didn't throw a fit.

This was an event that is engraved in Lai's mind to this day. I can only imagine that it messes with her head every now and then. Years later when I asked her about this incident she said, "I didn't know you guys were hiding because from where I was sitting in the open, I could still see almost everyone." This made us both laugh but uneasily.

* * *

By the afternoon of that same day we reached Thailand. I don't know how we finally crossed the border. All I can recall is waking up on the grounds of a Buddhist pagoda as Ath thrashed next to me. He was having a nightmare. In his sleep he shouted, "Where's the scarf, you motherfucker? I want the scarf!"

I rolled away from him so as to not get punched. My mother rushed over and pinned him down for he was trying to get up and run. When Ath calmed down and woke up, all he would say when my mother wanted to know about the dream was that he had a nightmare. He refused to say more and walked away, wanting to be left alone. I was rather pissed off at him for waking me up so frightfully.

The following day we left the temple for temporary shelter, recommended to us by one of my father's cousins. Like us, he was Nyaw but had become a Thai citizen when the French withdrew from Cambodia and a chunk of their former colony was annexed to Thailand. For about a month, we lived in a one-room wooden house that was attached to a much larger one. My parents, siblings, and I all crammed into this small space, except for Ai Sang Thout who chose instead to live with our grandmother. She wasn't that far from where we were, but still I'd wished he had been with us so we were all together.

Our house was small, but I thought it was lovely. Made of teak in a traditional Thai style, it had once been the maid's quarters. You rarely see such houses now, because so many have been torn down and replaced by modern ones. We rented the house from an elderly lady who lived on her own in the big house attached to our little one. We referred to her as *Mae Tao* (Grandma). It was customary for us to call an elderly woman "Grandma" even though we weren't related and didn't know much about her. She never left her house and rarely had visitors. The only time we saw her for more than a few seconds was when she introduced herself on the day we arrived. We thought it was rather sad that Mae Tao was by herself all the time. Our mother often reminded us to be quiet so Mae Tao could have her peace. Sometimes I wondered if she was still alive, because when Ath, Let, Lai, and I weren't making a racket fussing with each other, her house was so quiet you could hear a pin drop. Weird as it may seem, I sensed that Mae Tao was simply marking time, waiting for death to receive her.

Since this house was only a temporary home, we had absolutely nothing to do. Like most kids we were mischievous by nature and when bored found trouble. Which explains why one time Ath managed to convince me to do something unthinkable: he wanted me to mess with Lai just to test her strength. If he provoked her, he would get punished, because Lai was younger than him and a girl—all good reasons for him to assume that our parents would take Lai's side. However, in me Ath saw a little ally who would do what he asked and might just get away with it. He wasn't wrong. I was very happy to carry out his wish, instigated in the interest of stirring sibling rivalries.

It was a hot Sunday afternoon. Even though everyone was home, the house was quiet, too quiet. Ath, Let, Lai, and I tried to stay cool by lying on the wood floor, but then Ath slowly crawled on all fours toward me and whispered in my ear, "I dare you to kick Lai in the chin."

Bewildered, I shook my head no. Lai was strong. She would catch me in seconds and rip my bony body to pieces.

"Are you crazy? I'm scared!" I whispered back.

"I will protect you."

"How?" I asked.

"Just trust me," Ath said.

Despite my fears of Lai's wrath, I so desperately wanted someone to play with that I was gullible. So I found myself hesitantly walking up to Lai. She slowly sat up and looked at me, as if expecting me to say something, but instead I kicked her as instructed. Ath laughed when Lai yelped "ouch!" and rubbed her chin. Eyes blazing, she gasped in disbelief. Wary, I took a few steps back to see what Lai would do. Sure enough, she rushed at me like an angry tiger. Like captured prey wishing it could vanish, I braced for the attack, but Ath grabbed my hand and we dodged Lai just in time. We raced down the stairs toward the road. Lai ran after us until she tired herself out.

Ath and I stayed away from the house until dinnertime, hoping by then that Lai's anger would have subsided. When we returned, Let was waiting for us on the steps. She didn't want to miss seeing us get in trouble.

"They're here!" she yelled.

I hesitated to move any closer, but Ath didn't seem worried. I ducked behind him for fear that Lai would race out to attack me. Inside the house Mom, Let, and Lai stood in a line, ready to scold us. I thought to myself, *There's no way out of this one*, and I was prepared to put the blame on Ath. Mom, simmering with anger, towered over me, demanding answers.

"Why did you do it?" she snapped.

While we were hiding out, Ath and I hadn't practiced a confession, and since now that I was on the verge of tears, I said, "Ath told me to."

Ath didn't seem to mind that I turned him in.

"Yeah, they were whispering something, and then Mai kicked Lai in the chin," Let volunteered.

Standing next to Mom, Lai looked smug. Hands on hips, forehead wrinkled, my mother fastened a glare on Ath who did his best to look away. If looks could kill, this would be it for Ath.

"You should know better!" she screamed at Ath. He lowered his head. Mom turned to the rest of us, and I cringed as she shouted, "*Suu nee!* (You kids!)"

Whenever Mom vented her disappointment with us, it always began with this Nyaw expression, *suu nee*, and a long, exhaustive lecture followed—so long we wished she would spank us instead, although my mother never gave that kind of punishment.

Shoulders slumped, Let looked toward the door, Lai went from smiling to confused, and Ath seemed to shrink in size despite being both older and taller than the other two. For them, there was no way out of this scolding. As for me, shadowed by Ath, I snuck away unnoticed and hid behind a door. I vowed to never let Ath talk me into such a thing again. Ai Sang Thout would have never put me up to such mischief. My mother carried on and on with her lecture, reminding my siblings at length that we had just escaped with our lives, that we had no place to call home, and that we shouldn't make things more difficult than they already were.

The Farmhouse in Thailand

About a month later, we moved again, to a farm owned by my father's cousin. We would pay him rent and work the farm, a huge rice field that stretched as far as the eye could see. My grandmother and other relatives moved too, and we remained within walking distance of each other. Ai Sang Thout continued to live with our grandmother, but now he visited us at least once a week.

At the farmhouse my parents worked from sunup to sundown. When they weren't planting, tending or harvesting rice, my parents planted a vegetable garden, raised chickens, and hunted for game. Ath and Lai helped out in the rice field, or hunted or foraged for wild vegetables. Let stayed home to cook, clean, and care for the chickens. Everyone, except me, was always working. I hated having no one to play with and looked forward to the evening. After all the chores were done, Let and Lai allowed me to join them in whatever they were doing, as long as I wasn't a pest. It hadn't been forgotten, either, that I got them all into trouble when I kicked Lai. They didn't really trust me, but they put up with me so that Mom wouldn't give them a hard time. I needed their company, so I was happy just to be with them, even if I had to keep my mouth shut.

One nice quiet evening, Let, Lai, and I were sitting in our usual spot, under a tree on a hill that overlooked the house, when Let challenged me to steal a cigarette for her. She was barely eleven years old, but she managed to sneak a smoke here and there and would steal a cigarette from our father or uncles when an opportunity presented itself. We had no idea how she'd picked up this habit. Weirdly enough, Ath, Lai, and I never ratted her out to our parents.

"Dad always has cigarettes in his shirt pockets," Let said. I was suspicious. I thought this was how Let and Lai were hoping to get their revenge for my part in getting them into trouble. Where was Ath when I needed him?

"Why would I do that?" I challenged Let. Lai looked on and smirked as if to say, "Ha! What will do you now, little missy?"

"I'll let you have a puff," Let said. I contemplated her offer. I thought this might be a way to prove my loyalty to them. And I was enticed by the idea of trying something forbidden. A little later I nabbed one of Dad's cigarettes. Let was true to her word and let me have a puff on it. At the tender age of seven, I had my first taste of nicotine.

* * *

The closest neighbor to our isolated farmhouse was a cemetery no more than a city block away. Next to the cemetery was a field overgrown with evergreens. Since no one objected, we cleared that field and turned it into a vegetable garden. In no time we had yams, corn, and all kinds of herbs. At first I found it spooky that part of the garden led right into the cemetery, but we did what we had to do.

I would have thought that living next to a burial site would have me at my wit's end over ghosts and spirits. However, it didn't bother me as expected. The dead seemed at peace. Sometimes we roamed the cemetery to look for bamboo shoots, which were plentiful there. For me, it was more like a scavenger hunt, because I saw so many interesting items placed on top of the tombs to appease the spirit. What interested me the most was the rusty betel nut chew sets in the cemetery; every grandma I knew was well equipped with betel nut chew sets. Components of a betel set included a receptacle, either a box, a tray, or a basket; containers for the individual ingredients; and a cutter for slicing the nut or a bark. The three essential ingredients for chewing betel are betel leaf, limestone paste to spread on the leaf, and dried areca (betel) nut that has been thinly sliced. When combined these three ingredients are addictive and stimulating, which creates the feeling of a mild euphoria. It is an ancient custom, and my grandma and my mother depended on it daily. My father, on the other hand, chewed only the areca nut while chanting to cure a variety of illnesses. It was his way of practicing medicine. Judging by all of the betel chew set paraphernalia decorating so many graves, there were plenty of grandmas buried in that cemetery. Being very superstitious, my mother was adamant that we didn't disturb anything when we were there.

"You can look but don't touch anything," she reminded us every single time.

Despite living on a farm, food was scarce for our family, and we had to be resourceful to feed ourselves. Sweets were a very rare treasure. In our vegetable patch, my father, being one of those people who could grow anything, nourished baby Thai watermelons into sweet, tempting fruit. We didn't dare touch the melons, let alone pick one, without his permission. Only he knew when it was time and the best way to prepare his specialty dessert. He cut the melon into bite-size pieces, and then added condensed milk and coconut milk. Sometimes he added cooked tapioca; this way, he stretched the portions to be large enough for the whole family. I still remember the rich taste and lovely smell of that dessert, every bite of it satisfying my cravings for something sweet. I always licked the bowl clean. For me, these were heavenly moments.

On the other side of our farmhouse was a small pond that served no purpose. Being a practical man, my father decided to change that once it was the monsoon season. He bought some baby fish from town and released them into the pond. Several weeks later he bought some husks and strings with which to make a fishing pole.

"Follow me," he said to me one day.

I raced after him, grinning from ear to ear, delighted that someone was finally spending time with me. My happiness, though, was short lived. Dad pointed to an area of wet dirt beside the house, handed me a shovel, and said, "That's where you will find yourself some worms." Then he left.

I stood there, shovel in hand, disappointed with my father, and contemplating my next steps. I looked down at my feet, inspecting for any wriggly movement and ready to run if I saw any worms. I was so afraid of touching worms that I would have preferred to get stung by a scorpion, something that happened very often while I was asleep.

Luckily, Ath came to my rescue. He dug into the moist dirt, and in no time he collected half a can of worms. For the next week, I was sent off each morning to stick the fishing pole into the mud so the husks dropped into the water. Then, in the afternoon, I was to return and check the pole. Ath placed bait into the husks for me, and I did as I was told, but I only caught one small fish.

"Are you crazy? Fish couldn't survive in that tiny pond," Mom fussed to Dad after she saw how disappointed I was with my catch. After that I didn't have to go fishing again. Months later, the pond dried down to mostly ankle-deep mud. Ath suggested we forage for anything still alive in it, so together we created a mound of mud in the middle to divide the pond into two parts. Once that was done, we moved water from one side of the pond to the other using a bucket. To our delight we saw some fish wiggling around in the thick muck. We swooped into the mud and caught the fish with our hands. Once we had collected all the fish from the first side, we repeated the process for the other half. On such a hot and humid day, I didn't mind being covered by the cool mud. By the end of the day, we caught almost a dozen small fish.

A few weeks later, the hot weather dried the pond completely, creating cracks. Between the cracks Ath and I searched for frogs and went home with a handful of them. For dinner that evening, we ate stir-fried vegetables, crispy fried frogs, and a bowl of jasmine rice. It was delicious!

* * *

None of us could attend school in Thailand because we didn't have the proper documents for registration. As the youngest in the family, I didn't have work to do, so I had the luxury of sleeping into the morning. By the time I rose, my parents would have already spent half the morning in the rice field. The first thing I did every morning, even before I opened my eyes, was to sniff for the scent of fruit. Once or twice a week, my mother would put a piece of fruit next to our pillows before she left the house, either a banana or a mango. I treasured this simple gesture. To me, this was my mother's way of leaving a note that said she loved and hadn't forgotten about me.

One day, instead of eating the banana Mom left for me, I decided to save it for after dinner and hide it under my pillow. For the entire I day I kept a close eye on anyone who entered the room and didn't venture far from the house. About half a dozen times I checked the banana, making sure it was still there.

This will be the only time I will do this, I told myself because the worry was killing me.

At dinner that night, I ate very little because I knew I had something better waiting for me. As the others cleared their plates and cleaned up, I quietly left them and lay on my straw mat, excited, and pretended to be asleep. Even though it was a hot night, I covered myself in a blanket. When a covert peek from under the covers assured me that no one was looking, I took a big sniff of the sweet banana scent and carefully peeled back its skin. I savored every bite until it was nearly finished, and my enjoyment turned into disappointment. Determined to make the treat last a little longer, I nibbled around the last bit until only a small slimy piece was left. I pretended it was candy melting in my mouth, and that night I dozed off dreaming about banana-flavored candies.

The next day when Mom returned home from work she accused the others of playing a cruel joke on me.

"Remember, you kids need to be nice to each other," she warned us. All of us glanced at each other and thought, *"Now what?"*

"This morning I smelled something from Mai's mouth, and I discovered it was a piece of rotten banana. I know one of you put it there," she said and suspiciously glanced over at Ath, Let, and Lai. "She could have choked to death!" She gave each of them a hard stare. The others bit their lips. "It was a good thing I discovered it and threw it away," she continued.

Damn it, Mom, what a waste! I thought to myself.

The others grinned at each other, as if they were high-fiving. Amused and convinced that one of the others was responsible, they banked that if no one admitted anything no one would be punished. Sure enough, they kept quiet in support of each other. I didn't confess either and sat obediently next to Mom, trying to look as innocent as possible. Not only was I too embarrassed to admit that the banana was my own doing, but also it wasn't often that I received so much sympathy.

Friends and Foes

On a hot afternoon several months after we moved to the farm, a man approached the house. Seeing a stranger made everyone anxious. Dad stood on tiptoe for a better view. With one hand on her hip, Mom used the other to shield her eyes from the bright sunlight. She looked like she was saluting. Dad smiled when he recognized his oldest brother, my uncle Lee but his smile vanished as he took in his brother's grim expression. They had not been in contact since the Khmer Rouge came to power. In my father's mind churned dread of what had become of Uncle Lee's wife and three children. Mom hurried Uncle Lee to a seat in the shade. She would have collected his bag too, but he had none. He arrived only with the clothes on his back.

"Go get Uncle Lee some water," Mom said, her hands waving at us as if fanning away flies.

This was the first time I'd met Uncle Lee, and I liked him immediately. After a drink of water, he wiped the sweat from his forehead and told us that in his village the Khmer Rouge had begun taking away some of the men at night, and they were never seen again. The belief among the villagers was that the men were marched far into the forest and killed. One evening after returning from his work assignment, his wife told him there was a rumor that the Khmer Rouge would come for him that night. She told him to escape, which he did at that very moment. That was the last time Uncle Lee saw his wife and children and Cambodia. He crossed the border into Thailand and located our Thai cousin who directed him to our family.

"I knew you had escaped, and I knew our Thai cousin would know where you were," Uncle Lee explained. "This is how I found you." From that day onward, he was an addition to our family.

At the farmhouse it was common for me to overhear conversations about the war. There were always rumors about who was sick or who had been killed, and I began to have recurring nightmares. They always began at a beautiful beach or a river with white sand that felt good to my feet. I was always alone and strolling along the water when suddenly two paths would appear that led away from the water. I had to pick one without knowing what was at the end of either. Each time and whichever path I chose, halfway through the path, thorns appeared from everywhere, closed in, and captured me. A dark cloud would cast its shadow over me, and I would be engulfed by feelings of being alone and abandoned, like I was on the verge of passing out. I would burst awake from the dream, drenched in sweat and gasping for air.

A second version of the nightmare also took turns haunting me. This time the two paths in front of me were both clearly marked. One was smooth and inviting, and the other one was rough with spiky thorns everywhere. In the dream I wanted to go toward the smooth path but was pulled and sucked toward the unsmooth path, as if in a losing game of tug-of-war. My arms and legs would scramble for something to cling to, but with one zap I disappeared, taking my last breath with me. Jolted awake, I searched for Mom in the dark, scooting closer to her before I could drop off to sleep again. At least twice a week I battled these dreams.

It was not a happy time at the farmhouse although, for a while, I had a friend—a pet chicken I named Kagh. Unlike me, she was perfect, more like a special visitor friend from a faraway land who didn't belong with someone like me.

While I was beginning to show signs of malnourishment, pale and thin like a sick tree about to lose its bark, Kagh was plump and healthy with shiny, gold feathers that looked and felt like silk. She was flawless. In the back of my mind, I didn't think it was fair to her that she came into my life when she did. She belonged in a better place. I wished that she would take me away from the farmhouse and into her beautiful, peaceful world, not because I wanted to get away from my family, but because I didn't want to hear any more talk of war and death.

From the first moment I laid eyes on Kagh as a little chick, I loved her. She was from the first dozen chicks Dad brought from the market in our early days at the farm. I loved all the chicks, because they were adorable, sweet yellow fur balls with tiny beaks and tiny legs. The excited peeps they made when I fed them were music to my ears. For a few weeks the chicks followed me around like I was their mother. I gave them food and water and did a lot of running around with them. Soon they all became hens, and that was when Kagh and I became especially fond of each other, at least that was how I felt about her. In a lonesome house, she was my only companion and the one hen that never pecked for food too far from me. The other hens wandered off in search of better insects, but Kagh stayed nearby.

With Kagh I chatted about nonsensical stuff, and I loved that she seemed to nod in agreement with me much of the time. It was funny how she did two things at once, pecking the ground for insects and worms and listening to me. When she got bored with me, she would take a turn around the house but always circled back to where I was.

One day our cousin who owned the farm came to check on us as he usually did on a weekly basis. He was on the porch talking with Mom since Dad wasn't around.

"Mai, get your cousin a glass of water," my mother instructed. I left to do as I was told, but didn't have to go so far that I couldn't half-listen to her conversation with this cousin, a skinny, bald-headed man in his early forties.

As he got up to leave, he made a startling request. "I would like a bird to take home for dinner," he said to Mom, pointing at Kagh.

If I could have, I would have wrapped myself around him like a mighty python and squeezed the life out of him. My mother must have sensed what I was thinking for she shot me a warning look.

Assuming a subservient demeanor, my mother smiled at our cousin and said, "Mai is very attached to that hen; please take another one."

Our cousin didn't comment on Mom's suggestion, but I'd already made up my mind that I did not like this skinny old man. He was cold, distant, and from him there was never a gentle word. As a matter of fact, I don't recall him ever speaking to me.

Obviously her suggestion didn't sit well with him, for this cousin went home empty-handed with his head held high like he was superior to the rest of us. I watched his shiny head grow smaller in the distance to make sure that he was good and gone. A part of me wished that he would vanish forever.

I didn't trust this cousin, and I made a mental note to be around whenever he showed up. However, time passed, and I forgot about his weekly visit. When he next came, I wasn't at home. When I returned, Kagh was gone.

"Why?" I cried to my mother.

She didn't offer any explanation, just said, "Here's eighty baht (about $2) that he gave you for it."

"I don't want his money!" I slapped the money out of the way and rushed to get away from her.

I felt like I had let Kagh down, and I mourned for her like I would mourn for a human being. It was the first time in my life that I felt utterly defeated.

After Kagh was gone, a rooster began to torment me. He was a feisty little fellow, that rooster. It all started one morning while I was in the yard picking some red peppers, and the rooster knocked me off balance. It took me a little while to realize what had just happened. I was stunned that something that small (with feathers!) could have come at me that hard. The rooster ran off, and I thought then that maybe he had just bumped into me by accident. But no, he was preparing to attack me again. He took his position a few feet from me, lifted his wings, and hurtled himself at me again full force! To fend him off, I threw chili peppers and swung a bunch of green onions at him. I was sure he knew these defenses were harmless green onions and chili peppers, since he showed no sign of backing down. I raced up the stairs to get away from him.

"What's all that commotion?" someone asked.

"The rooster is after me!" I cried. From within the house, somebody chuckled.

"You're encouraging him when you run away like that," Ath advised coolly, as if rooster attacks were an everyday thing.

"It's your fault," I shot back. "If you hadn't taken him to a cockfight last week, he wouldn't have acted like that."

"He didn't even get a chance to fight."

"It doesn't matter. It did something to him and now he's angry."

For the next week, that rooster was a nightmare. When he wasn't chasing me, he tormented the hens and crippled the chicks. Dad reached his limits with the bird. He didn't plan to kill the rooster, just teach it a lesson. But the stick Dad used landed heavy on its neck, and the rooster was down.

He squawked his last curse, "Gaa!" and went silent.

Tragedies

Forever etched in my mind is the day we learned Ai Sang Thout was missing.

Everyone was home on a Saturday afternoon doing one thing or the other. I was on the ground floor of the house talking to an invisible cricket friend, confined to a tiny grass basket that Ath had made me earlier that day, when our cousin Ta arrived at our house. We didn't have many visitors, so Ath, Let, Lai, and I were excited to see our cousin.

We ran to greet him, but Cousin Ta sped past us without a hello, only a frantic demand. "Where's Uncle and Auntie?" He didn't even wait for our reply.

"What happened?" we called after him and tried to catch up.

My parents calmly emerged from the house, but cousin Ta's waving hands and breathless shouts alarmed them. They rushed to meet him, and the three of them huddled underneath the stilted house.

Minutes later, Dad and Mom raced up the steps and inside. I heard a big commotion of things being tossed around. We ran to them, asking what was going on.

"Your brother is missing, and we need to go find him," my father said.

The news knocked the wind out of me. In my head I shouted that it couldn't be true, that it had to be a dream, but seeing my mother's pale face only escalated my growing panic. I followed her around the house as she dashed from one corner to the other gathering what they would need. Tears filled my eyes.

Mom turned to me and said, "I don't need this right now, Mai." I held on to her sarong, but she nudged me out of the way.

My parents set off with Cousin Ta to search for Ai Sang Thout. My siblings and I were confused and stunned. Our eyes followed the three bodies as they got smaller and smaller until they disappeared altogether.

Once they were gone, I don't remember any of us speaking. Maybe we did, maybe not. I couldn't listen to anyone. I couldn't even bring myself to look their way. For the very first time in my life, I wanted to be alone.

We did nothing the rest of the day, not even our chores. Instead we wandered about aimlessly and waited for news, checking the road at every sound for the sign of someone, anyone, coming. Day became night. I don't remember eating or sleeping, just waiting for what seemed like an eternity, praying a lot, and hoping this horrific waking nightmare would end.

Around noon the next day, the sight of two people, not three, heading toward us made me feel as if I had been stabbed in the chest, had torn out my heart, and ripped it into pieces.

It is true. The Khmer Rouge will eventually take everything from me, I said to myself while fighting to hold back my tears.

We reluctantly gathered around my parents to hear what they had to say. Mom was pale, like someone whose sorrow had sucked the life out of her. Head lowered, she staggered inside the house alone. We didn't dare approach her. Quietly, we moved closer to Dad, our eyes searching his for answers.

Finally Ath found the courage to break the silence and begged our father to tell us what had happened. As Dad told us the story, we sat quietly, listening with our heads lowered, sniffling.

"In SaKeo, Thailand, a town that borders Cambodia and Thailand, Cousin Ta and Ai Sang Thout went hunting. Ai Sang Thout was climbing a tree in search of honey, when Cousin Ta saw a few Khmer Rouge soldiers appear from the jungle. He called out to Ai Sang Thout, who must not have heard him because he continued to climb toward the top, as if he had all the time in the world. He didn't once look down but kept his sight focused on the beehive at the very top of the tree. Cousin Ta heard shots and the bullets nearly hit him. He ran for cover, hoping the soldiers didn't notice Ai Sang Thout in the tree. That was when Cousin Ta ran all the way to our house," Dad said. He shook his head in disbelief. "By the time we reached the tree where your brother was last seen, there wasn't a soul there. The whole area seemed undisturbed, and the tree your brother climbed stood alone."

My father continued to say there was no trace of blood, not even a piece of clothing, and no sign of struggle. They think that Ai Sang Thout must have obeyed the soldiers' orders to leave with them into the jungle.

We were speechless for the rest of the afternoon. Ath, Let, and Lai dispersed to find their own comfort. There was no way to be with Mom. She kept to herself, pretending to be busy but constantly using her sarong to wipe her face. She averted her gaze the few times I looked her way, searching for a sign from her to welcome me, but I didn't get any. It was very difficult for me to see her that way, and my heart ached even more. I was beyond sad and couldn't fathom what she was going through. I wanted to comfort her, but as a kid I didn't know how. So I left her alone.

Dad, on the other hand, was composed. He did odd jobs around the house, fixed things that were broken, and told Let what to make for dinner. This was the way he was taught to be under such circumstances. It was not until later that evening that I noticed he seemed withdrawn. From the silence I thought he was asleep, but he wasn't. He stared at an empty wall without blinking, leaning against a pile of pillows for support, his right arm resting on his forehead. His expression was neither sad nor happy but deep in thought, like Buddhists meditating. Dad remained as he was for hours into the night, almost as if he was in a trance. It was the first time I saw my father like that, and I have seen him in such a state many times since. I knew what it meant, though, and I dared not disturb him.

As for me, that afternoon I escaped to a grassy area of the house, sat down, and beat the grass with my fists. Choking with tears, in my head I screamed, W*hy!?*

For the first few hours, I fooled myself by musing about Ai Sang Thout's return. I thought maybe he would return to us the following day or sometime in the coming weeks or months or years. Death was a strange concept. In my head I rode an emotional roller coaster and grappled with difficult questions: is there another world; will Ai Sang Thout reincarnate to another family or back into our family? Then, in small ways, I blamed Ai Sang Thout for leaving me. I went back and forth so much in my head that by the end of the day I went from confused to numb.

A month came and went, but there was no sign of Ai Sang Thout. Mom and Dad were so desperate that they consulted a monk at the temple. To predict Ai Sang Thout's fate, the monk tried balancing a stick on the floor. Since the stick balanced well, the monk predicted that Ai Sang Thout could possibly be alive, but he advised us to perform a death ceremony for Ai Sang Thout anyway, in case he was no longer on this earth. That way his spirit would be free.

Two weeks later the monks came to our house to conduct the ritual. Our house was crowded with relatives. The room was simply decorated, with one side reserved for the monks and the other side for family. In the middle my parents had placed food and new clothes prepared as an offering to the spirit of Ai Sang Thout. At midmorning the ceremony began. Incense filled the room as the monks began chanting the mantra. Together the mantra and the incense floated slowly away from the house. The ceremony lasted for almost an hour. The mood was calm as everyone obediently sat on the floor facing the monks with palms clamped together, listening attentively to the chanting. Mom and Dad's expression was neither sad nor happy. To them, this was the right way to end our loss. For that moment, the ceremony brought some kind of closure and gave my parents some peace of mind.

For me, though, it was too confusing. Since Ai Sang Thout went missing, every night before going to bed I cursed the Khmer Rouge in my prayers. Whenever my hunger for revenge reared strong, I closed my eyes. I could see silhouettes of men in black uniforms with red scarves, and I would play out the dark thoughts that consumed me.

* * *

Our losses didn't end with the disappearance of Ai Sang Thout. About a month and half later one of our cousins suddenly became very ill and died. This cousin had been one of my playmates back in Cambodia, and his death saddened me. Since our escape to Thailand, I had only seen him once and briefly.

My mother refused to let us attend the funeral, so for us there was no way to say good-bye to him.

"You will stay home. There's no need for you to be at the funeral, and I don't want to hear any of you complain." Mom said.

She did what she thought was best for us under the circumstances, but since we lived near the cemetery, we could not miss the funeral entirely. We could view the parade from a distance. The weather was hot and humid that afternoon, and the house was too silent. Usually the chickens ran around making noise, but that day they were quiet, as if they mourned too. As I watched my relatives slowly following the coffin across the rice field, dry and bare from its recent harvesting, a noise coming from underneath me distracted my attention. I looked down to see Let and Lai creeping out from underneath the house. Let sat on the only chair we had, and Lai leaned against the house pole. Both of them peered off in the direction of the funeral parade. Then I spotted Ath sitting on a tree branch doing the same. The sight of the wooden coffin at the front of the line of mourners is still vivid in my mind.

During this time, death and illness became a regular event. One Sunday while my parents were off working somewhere, my sisters and I were resting in our usual spot under a tree near the house. Let and Lai talked while I sat on the side half-listening. Ath tended the neighbor cows in the next field. All of a sudden we heard an explosion. We paused, looked at each and then in the direction where we thought the blast might have come from. Never before had we heard such an explosion. Ten minutes later, just as the sound of it was out of our minds, we heard a man running in our direction, shouting and gesturing at us, but we couldn't hear or make out what he was saying. As he drew closer, we recognized the man as our neighbor. Panting, he asked for the whereabouts of our parents.

"They're not here!" we shouted.

"Then which way to your great aunt's house?"

We all pointed in that direction and asked why.

"Her son just had a bad accident. He stepped on a land mine!" His voice trailed off as he rushed off to our aunt's house. My body became rigid, my jaw tightened, and my mind filled with horrible images. I pictured my cousin's body exploded in all directions, legs flying in a nearby bush, arms dangling from a tree branch, and the rest of his body scattered here and there in the dirt. I was so consumed by this vision that I swore I smelled the burned flesh of my cousin, just sixteen years old, young, handsome, strong, and vibrant. He had been taking care of the cows, like most boys his age, when the accident happened.

His family had escaped from Cambodia at the same time we had, and they lived in the same place as my grandmother. Every time this cousin passed our house he stopped for a visit, saying hello to whoever was home but never staying too long and become a nuisance. He was kind, cheerful, and a free spirit. Whenever he passed by our house in the evening, it was common to hear him singing his heart out. He had a beautiful voice, and I often found myself humming to the same tune for the rest of the night. Upon learning that he had died, one of my first thoughts was that I wouldn't hear him sing anymore.

The following day I overheard my parents discussing the price of kerosene. Without thinking I asked what the kerosene was for.

Either Let or Lai, I can't recall which one, gave me an evil glare and scolded, "It's for cremation, and next time don't ask such a stupid question!"

Truly I wish I hadn't asked, because I didn't like the thought of cremation. I went to bed that night thinking about how the flames would melt the flesh from my cousin's body, and I prayed and prayed that he wouldn't feel any pain.

That night I dreamed I was alone, standing under the usual tree where I saw my great aunt pass by carrying a yellow tin can of kerosene. She was by herself and heading toward the burial site. In the dream I didn't want to disturb her, so I neither waved nor called out to her. This sight of her alone was so sad to me. I became weak in the knees. I had no will power to fight it, so I slumped to the ground. I felt the cool earth, and I had no desire to move. I sat there for a very long time, until I woke from the morning sun. All that morning I felt like I was still in my dream.

Memories of Ai Sang Thout

Although my memories of my brother are few, I treasure the ones I have. They've replayed in my head a million times. It is the recollection of the bond between us during our frightening journey to Thailand that I cherish the most, but there are other memories.

I remember a year before the Khmer Rouge upended our lives when Ai Sang Thout was a novice. For almost a year, like most boys his age at that time, he lived at the temple and was schooled by the monks. He was the first in our family to go through this important ritual, and my parents were overjoyed that their eldest son completed this rite of passage.

I can clearly recall the ceremony that marked his commencement as a novice. The monks came to our house to conduct it, and family, cousins, and friends packed in to celebrate the birth of Ai Sang Thout's manhood. The monks chanted, and everyone else held their palms together to show respect as they listened to the chanting. After this, Ai Sang Thout's robe was neatly packed for its return to the temple, as another novice would soon wear it, and he was given a present of new clothes. He said very little as we honored him. Since then he had always embodied for me everything that was pure and righteous. I was proud to be his little sister.

Any moment with Ai Sang Thout was a treasure for me. I jumped up and down and was so excited whenever he asked me to join him for anything. I remember my first bike-riding experience with him. I didn't know where the bike came from, or who it belonged to. For certain, it wasn't ours.

"Please, Mom, can I?" I begged her. She was busy preparing lunch.

"That's just too dangerous. I don't think you should," she said absentedmindedly, without even looking up.

Ai Sang Thout winked at me, took my hand, and led me to the front of the village where I saw the bike waiting for us.

"I'll put you on the back," he told me as he lifted me onto a tiny seat.

I'd never sat on a bike before, and I felt so high off the ground. I gripped Ai Sang Thout's arms until they appeared to turn white.

"Mai," he said, "you have to let me go for a second so that I can position myself. After that you can put your arms around my waist."

He unpeeled my hands that were glued to his arms and turned his back toward me. Quickly I refastened my arms around his waist, and we took off. We rode around several times, hit a few things, and fell over more than once, but Ai Sang Thout always managed to catch me, no matter how far I bounced off the bike.

From this I learned to trust Ai Sang Thout. I trusted him when he sat me on the back of the bull without a saddle and nothing to hold onto, even though Mom and everyone else told him not to do it. I clung to the bull's back with both my arms and my legs. For the life of me, I couldn't steady myself and sit up like the other kids. Instead, lightweight that I was, I kept sliding. Ai Sang Thout ran from one side of the bull to the other, trying to help me sit upright, but it didn't work, much to the amusement of everyone watching, myself included.

The last time I saw Ai Sang Thout was when he did his weekly visit to the farmhouse after our escape from Cambodia. Normally his visits were short, but this time he stayed much longer and spent most of it playing with me. I rode on his back, and he pretended to be different animals, from roaring tigers to a bear and its cub. After we got tired of that, we lay side by side on the ground looking at the clear blue sky, and every now and then he sniffed my cheeks. This was one of those rare times I felt at peace while we lived at the farmhouse, and it made me smile for days afterward. Whenever I want to remember Ai Sang Thout, what he looked like and how he was, this is the memory I return to.

PART II

IN BETWEEN

Camp Life

A few months after Ai Sang Thout disappeared, the situation in Cambodia grew worse by the day. Those who could took the risk and fled to Thailand. The stream of refugees prompted international organizations to set up a camp in Aranyaprathet, Thailand. Within a few days of hearing about the camp, my father and some cousins went to scout it out. When he returned, he told us we would move there in a few weeks.

We had been living in Thailand without permission for almost a year and had to keep our presence very hush-hush. At any given moment, the Thai authorities could appear on our doorstep, asking to see our papers. Fearing harassment and the threat of being sent back to Cambodia, the camp offered us sanctuary. We would still be at the mercy of someone else, but at least we could safely claim our identity and declare our presence.

The prospect of having a camp full of playmates thrilled me, but I was even more over the moon when I heard that I could attend school in the camp. If it were up to me, I would have had us leave that farmhouse and all the sad memories attached to it—Kagh, Ai Sang Thout, my cousins—that day. However, it wasn't until sometime in the fall of 1976 that once again our family and relatives packed our few belongings and relocated to a small, thatched roof house in the camp.

We lived in the Aranyaprathet camp for about three years. Nyaw people called this camp Soon Alan. It was just a stone's throw from the Cambodian border, and it housed no more five hundred families. Our family was in the first group to move there. At the entrance of the camp stood some brick buildings that housed the administration offices and one of the schools, the one I attended, plus a big open area. Behind the school was another brick building, the hospital, and beyond that was the heart of the camp, the market. Living quarters, also made of brick, surrounded the market and the hospital. A second and bigger school, built from wood, and the camp's only playground were located near the back entrance of the camp. Sandwiched between all the brick buildings, were the rows and rows of small thatch huts that housed the refugees. The camp was small, about the size of a golf course, so it didn't take long for me to know my way around it. I knew which part I was to avoid, as instructed by my mother, because it was dangerous, and which part I was allowed to roam. Roaming, however, was limited. We were not allowed to leave the boundaries of the camp without first getting permission. Unlike refugee camps you see in movies, the camp I was in had no barbed wire fences, just mounds of dirt piled to mark the borders of the enclosure. There were watchtowers on some of the mounds that were manned by Thai guards, at least for a while. For some reason the guards abandoned the towers after only a month.

Soon the kids in the camp turned the towers into a place to hang out. My cousin friends and I spent many hours playing house inside the towers, although at night, apparently, they were rendezvous spots for lovers. Compared to the huts we lived in, the watchtowers were very nice. It looked a lot like a patio with a picnic table inside. I especially liked the watchtower roofs because they seemed like they were built to last, whereas the roof of our hut was made of dried palm leaves that needed replacing every year. Otherwise we would be soaked during the monsoon season. To make matters worse, the palm leaves were infested with bugs and scorpions. I didn't mind the bugs so much, especially those that didn't bite, but I hated the scorpions that bit me during my sleep. It was no surprise that I often woke to find a terrible red welt somewhere on my body.

The guards, dressed in military uniforms, switched from doing surveillance from the towers to strolling the streets, corners, and allies. I don't recall if they had guns, but they all carried batons as they strolled the camp in heavy, black combat boots. I'd never seen such gigantic boots.

My siblings and I didn't spend as much time together once we moved to the camp, because we each formed our own group of friends, some of whom were our cousins. Prior to the camp, Ath was the only one who would play with me when time allowed, and he defended me when Let and Lai ganged up on me, as they occasionally did. He was now in his preteens though, and preferred to be with his many camp friends and preferred to do guy things. I had plenty of cousin friends of my own, so his absence didn't bother me. Overall, Ath took to life in the camp with ease. He was a good kid and didn't make much trouble for Dad or Mom.

I also stopped shadowing Let and Lai, which didn't bother them in the slightest. They were still close though and would get themselves in and out of trouble together. Let always got the both of them in trouble with her motormouth, and Lai got beat up a few times—by our cousin friends, of all people—for defending her. That was the way it was with them: Lai played policewoman and protected Let. I played the bystander afraid to do anything.

* * *

When we first moved into the camp, there was no market to buy food. We received all our food from the international aid organizations. During our first month, Thai people brought goods to sell. Because none of the refugees had *baht*, the Thai currency, we traded gold for goods that were in turn sold to fellow refugees. That was how the camp market came to be. In time it became a vibrant place that sprang to life twice per day—at dawn and late afternoon/early evening. In addition to having many playmates, the market was one of the other things I loved about life in the camp that first year. For families with little means, it served an essential purpose, as we could buy all kinds of fruits, vegetables, seafood, poultry, pork, beef, and spices. Other stalls sold clothes, medicines, accessories, music, and electronics. There was even a salon. The market brought liveliness to the camp, and for some it brought a livelihood back into their lives. It became the place for young people to mingle, for older folks to inquire about this or that, and where everyone gossiped, spread their rumors, and received their news.

In the camp I had my first encounters with *falang,* the word for Westerners in Nyaw, Thai, and Lao. With the exception of the translators, all of the aid workers were *falang.* Their physical appearance fascinated me—the colors of their skin, hair, and eyes. I wondered what made their skin so light and if it meant they were cleaner than I was. For a while I scrubbed extra hard during my bath. Their silken blond hair didn't seem real to me, but I wanted to touch it and see how it felt compared to my own. At first the variation in their eye colors unnerved me. As far as I knew, only cats could have different colors for their eyes. I once heard that cats were wandering spirits, so I avoided eye contact with the *falang* as much as I could. When they weren't looking my way though, I spied on them.

All of the men aid workers wore beards, something I was not particularly fond of. I liked to read a person's face, and the beards were like a mask that prevented me from doing so. The *falang* women were more intriguing to me anyway, so it was no problem for me to keep my distance from the men. Nonetheless, I was very curious about why the *falang* men were very tall and hairy. Next to them I felt like a midget. When I asked my mother why that was so, she offered a bizarre theory.

"In the old days," she said, "*falang* people were giants with lots of hair! They were even bigger and hairier back than. Eventually, they shrank to the size that they are now."

Her explanation made my hair stand on end. "Really, Mom?"

"Yes!" she exclaimed without hesitation. My grandmother nodded in agreement.

I was confused. I knew giants to be evil, but I saw that the *falang* were not. Luckily, my mother's theory didn't stop the admiration I felt for the aid workers, especially the ladies who were always friendly, warm, and all smiles. I became fixated on all things Western and wanted so much to be like them that I often pretended to be one, and went to wild lengths to transform myself. To attain a rosy complexion, I collected pink flowers and smashed them in the palm of my hand until they formed a smooth paste that I applied to my lips and cheeks. Or I placed flat rocks between the heels of my feet and my flip-flops, and then tied a rope around my foot to hold the rock in place. Then I wobbled around inside the watchtower, pretending I wore high-heeled shoes and lived in my large house on the hill with a beautiful view of the city and a sturdy roof.

"No scorpion will bother me now!" I announced to the world.

I was so infatuated with the Western world that I believed it was the world that my pet chicken, Kagh, was from. And, of course, that was a world I wanted to be in.

* * *

I remember the first New Year celebration in the camp. It brought color and excitement and happiness to people who had been in limbo since fleeing the war. The ladies dressed in their best traditional clothes, wore bright red lipstick, and put flowers in their hair; the scent of perfume trailed after them as they passed by. As the evening of the celebration approached, everyone milled about with anticipation.

The celebration was held in the main courtyard at the front of the camp, just before the gate to the outside world. For the entertainment there was an outdoor movie, a *Morlum* concert, and a *lamvong*. The movie was a mixed success: being held outside it was too noisy for anyone to hear, and it was in Thai, a language not all Cambodians understood. Still, New Year was a reason to celebrate no matter what, and the *morlum* concert was a favorite of the Nyaw.

Morlum, originally from Laos, is similar to blues, rhythm and blues, or soul music in America. It's done on a Laotian instrument called a *Kaen*, but it has an Afrocentric backbeat. Sometimes *morlum* is improvised, but essentially it tells stories of love and hardship experienced by country people, hence, its popularity with the Nyaw.

Ever since I could remember, a celebration wasn't a celebration without a Lao/Cambodian folk dance called *lamvong*. Both Lao and Cambodians claim the dance to be their own, although the origins of it aren't clear. The dancers move continuously in a circle, gracefully moving their arms and legs and bending their fingers.

As I watched the concert and the dancers that night, my first New Year celebration outside of Cambodia, I thought of Ai Sang Thout. I wondered where he was and what was he doing at that very moment. Whenever thoughts of him occurred, I always kept them to myself. Since moving to the camp, no one spoke of Ai Sang Thout, at least not to me.

Getting By

By our second year in the Aranyaprathet camp, the refugee population had doubled, and so had the number of security guards. Because our camp was too small, a second one called Camp Khao I Dang was built. It was much bigger than ours. As more and more Cambodians arrived in Thailand, they were housed in Khao I Dang, and they arrived in a far worse condition than we had.

Meanwhile, in our camp, without any work available, the refugees became desperate for money. People began to sneak out of the camp to look for work with the Thais in the area. My family's circumstances were no different as our budget and food began to run low. My mother asked for permission to return to the farmhouse in Thailand. Since we had worked on the farm and paid our cousin rent, she wanted to bring back a sack of rice. It never occurred to her that our cousin might refuse. But he did, and she returned to the camp fuming as she told us about the incident.

When our cousin, the same cousin who took Kagh from me, saw Mom with a sack of rice, he asked her rudely, "What do you think you are doing with that sack?"

"I would like to have it," my mother answered.

"You may not have it. Now go away!" he said, waving his hand for her to go.

Before leaving in tears, to his face my mother cursed him to Buddha, the ultimate curse one Buddhist could say to another, "Buddha is my witness and he will judge you!" My father was displeased with what she had said. "Isn't that too much? You shouldn't have said that to him," he told her. Mom gave him an evil glare and continued to vent her anger. It was a difficult time, and every grain of rice was counted. This incident was the first of the many times that I would be reminded how precious rice was to my family. Even before the war, my family farmed rice because our survival depended on it. I must admit that the value of rice remains ingrained in me to this day. My family still keeps a stash of rice, enough to feed an army.

At that time what money we had was spent only on food and medicine. Thanks to my father's ability to be frugal, he kept us all fed, and none of his children went a day without food. My dad always cared for us and 100 percent of the time put us first before himself. For instance, when it came to food, he saved the best pieces of meat for us, be it pork, beef, or fish. He would nibble on the bones or the broth or the vegetables, and put the pieces of meat on our plates. Despite my father's efforts, after a while we began to show signs of malnourishment. Let's stomach ballooned. Lai's hair turned reddish blonde, a change I thought was pretty because it made her look more like the *falang* ladies I admired. That change in Lai's hair, though, was the result of a nutritional deficiency. Ath and I became somewhat emaciated, not unlike the Jewish prisoners in the Nazi concentration camps.

Somehow, though, every New Year Ath, Let, Lai, and I each received a set of new clothes and a pair of flip-flops. Our sarongs were almost always identical—plain black or dark blue on top with a strip of colorful pattern at the bottom, and a plain shirt to go with it. The day after the New Year, with the exception of our size, Let, Lai, and I walked around the camp looking like triplets. Ath got a pair of pants and a simple shirt. We took extra care of our new clothes so they would last until the following year. By New Year the clothes from the previous year were raggedy. These then became cleaning cloths. By the time I attended school in the camp, I had two outfits: one for playing and the school uniform that Lai had outgrown and passed on to me.

As poor as we were, I remember my mom wanted her hair done like the rest of the ladies in the camp.

"I'm thinking about getting a perm," she said to my father nonchalantly one day, to test the waters.

"If you want to, go ahead," he said to her. Mom paused. She wanted the perm, but she didn't want the family to fall short because of the expense. Her cousin friends convinced her to get the perm anyway.

I went with her to the camp salon the day of her appointment. This salon wasn't like a beauty salon you would find in the States. It was in someone's cramped apartment. Inside sat two other ladies with rollers on their heads waiting patiently. Mom was the third customer. She walked in hesitantly. I followed her, feeling skeptical about the whole business. Inside the tiny room, the smell of chemicals was overpowering and burned my nostrils. Beauty supplies were stacked from floor to ceiling in one corner, and I took in the array of colorful nail polishes, makeup, and hair chemicals. The other corners of the little room were reserved for the kitchen and sleeping areas. In the space that remained, there was just enough room to squeeze in three customers. In the background, Cambodian music blared at full volume. The beautician who greeted us with a broad smile was a middle-aged lady. With her dark complexion and full lips painted with bright red lipstick, I thought she was very pretty. Like most salespeople I've met, she seemed overly nice.

After Mom settled in, the other ladies made small talk with her, but she said very little back. Mom rarely spoke Cambodian and was shy about it when she did, so it was a good thing I was there to keep her company. Two hours later, my mother's new hairdo was finished. I felt lightheaded from the chemicals and was happy to be leaving. Mom gave off that same chemical smell all day long, and I kept my distance from her for the rest of the day. Mom said very little about her new hairdo, and I've never found out if she liked the results of her trip to the salon or not. As for me, once the chemicals cleared from my head, I liked her new look.

* * *

One of the biggest buildings in the camp was the hospital. I went there a few times for vaccinations but never when I was sick. Dad was the family healer and always the primary person to deal with any kind of illness. If his methods didn't work, there were other home remedies. If those failed, Dad bought medicines at the market and treated us at home.

It was at the camp that I experienced my first serious illness. At first I simply felt weak, but within days I couldn't eat anything. When I tried, the food came out from both ends. For four days I lay ill. On the afternoon of the fifth day, everything went dark. My mother shook me gently to try to wake me. I heard her but couldn't move, talk, or open my eyes. Then I felt the bamboo sticks of my mat vibrate. I knew then that a crowd had rushed in and gathered around me. I heard more frantic voices, mumbo jumbo, and people telling each other what was needed to cure me. It was chaos.

Dad chanted, and I felt a cool breeze and specks of wetness as he spat betel juice on me. Someone began parting pieces of my hair, tugging and pulling at it. I wanted to say how wonderful that felt and ask for it not to stop, but I couldn't form the words.

Next someone rolled me over, and I smelled Tiger Balm. I thought, *Oh no! Not the Tiger Balm!* I knew what that meant, and I felt the coins rubbing on my back seconds later.

Coining is an ancient remedy practiced by the people in that part of the world. The method is applied to an area of the body, such as the chest, back, or shoulders. The technique uses coins to rub on the skin vigorously until the skin appears deep red or bruised. Doing this allows a path for the bad wind to be released from the body. The wind is the cause of the illness, and when the wind is released, the person feels better.

After the Tiger Balm was applied all over my back, two people worked the coins, starting at my shoulders. One person coined the right side of my back, and the other coined the left, working along the outline of each vertebra until the skin looked bruised. Then they moved on to the next vertebra. The rubbing with the coin was so painful that it was hard for me to breathe. I was hurting, and I managed to twitch a muscle to let them know. I heard someone say, "*Coy coy daa.*(Gently please.)" The coining finally stopped at my lower back. *Thank goodness,* I told myself. A few minutes later, my sarong was peeled from my body and replaced with a fresh one. Apparently I had dirtied myself at the end of the coining, which was very embarrassing.

By the following morning I was mobile again. When Lai saw me, she said, "Your back looks like a skeleton."

"Don't worry," my mother hurried to say, as she saw tears in my eyes. "It will disappear in a few weeks."

Mom School, Camp School

Most of the children in the camp attended one of its two Thai schools. For those who could afford it, private lessons in English and French were taught by some of the refugees in their homes. The camp schools, however, were free. So Let, Lai, and later I took advantage of them. Because of my age, I only went to school during the last six months we lived in the camp. For the first two and a half years, while the other children went to their lessons, I spent my days receiving lessons on life from my mother.

My mother was everything to me. She was the love that I longed for, the air that I breathed, and the food that nourished my soul. She was my safety blanket, and I couldn't go a day without her. Like most kids I believed everything that my mom taught me, but some of the lessons she tried to teach me didn't sink in until years later.

Allow me to share with you a story that involved chicken feet. One evening while living at the camp, our family was having *kaeng kai* (chicken soup) for dinner. We all sat in a circle on the floor. As always, my place in the circle was next to Mom. As she spooned soup into bowls, I noticed chicken feet floating on the surface of the soup. However, into my bowl of warm jasmine rice, Mom added only broth and a piece of boneless meat. Bored, I ate my soup while observing Dad, Uncle Lee, and Ath eating the chicken feet. They all seemed to enjoy cracking the bones with their teeth. The sucking sounds they made were annoying, but I was curious as to what the bony feet tasted like. To my surprise, I reached over and spooned a foot from the soup bowl onto my plate. The room went silent.

The lifeless foot rested on my plate with its rigid claws pointing upward. It was hard to the touch with no obvious trace of meat. I was taking my time, contemplating how I should attack the foot.

Mom looked at me from the corner of her eye and said with great seriousness, "You know, Mai, if you eat that chicken foot, you will steal someone else's husband when you grow up."

This made me pause. Dad, Uncle Lee, and Ath glanced my way to see what I would do while Let and Lai tried to hide their giggles.

"You see the claws on the chicken feet? They are waving for someone's husband to come to you," Mom said as she demonstrated by shaping her hand into a claw and pulling at my raggedy shirt.

Blushing, I pushed Mom's hand away. Let and Lai held their stomachs and were about to fall over from laughter.

"It is not a good virtue for a young lady to do this to the wife, so a young girl shouldn't eat such a thing," Mom said in closing.

"Can you eat mine, please?" I asked my father.

"All right," he agreed.

When I was sixteen years old, it finally dawned on me what she had been trying to do when she rescued me from those chicken feet. She had understood that it was tough for a kid to eat something like that. Besides, lacking any nutritional value, there was no benefit to my eating them. When Mom had filled my bowl and gave me the boneless piece of meat, she had given me the best she had to offer. As mothers do.

As much as I loved spending time with my mother, I could not wait to attend school. Located at the front of the camp, my school consisted of two buildings adjacent to each other. It was the area that least resembled the stark realities of camp life. It was clean and surrounded by all sorts of flowers and decorative bushes. I liked the jubilant sounds of the kids playing. We were guarded by teachers dressed in white shirts and dark blue skirts rather than soldiers with sticks and boots. Every morning we stood in line to salute the Thai flag and sing the Thai national anthem. After that, the two Thai teachers meticulously inspected us from head to toe and reminded us about the importance of good hygiene, and to brush our teeth, wash daily, and maintain a clean school uniform. If anyone didn't meet these standards, they received a spanking on their palm, one smack for each infraction.

I had heard reports about my teacher even before I started school.

"If you have her as your teacher, you're doomed," a few of my cousin friends warned.

On my first day of school, when I learned I was in this teacher's class, I thought I was the unluckiest girl. My palms became sweaty, and I kept one eye on the door, hoping the day would end fast. I went home wishing that a mistake had been made, and the next morning it would be discovered that I was meant to be with the other teacher. During my first week of school, I did everything possible to avoid my teacher, but as time passed I decided that I liked her and that the rumors about her were mistaken. She was strict but very fair. I sensed that she understood our situation in the camp and what was happening around her. I also sensed that she liked me too, and in the end she made my first school experience a happy one.

Time Moves On

By 1979 the camp began to look like a ghost town, because many refugees had emigrated to the United States, France, or Canada. We witnessed and said many farewells to friends, neighbors, and relatives. In this same year, though, a mass of Cambodian refugees poured into Thailand. Unlike the previous waves of people, the latest influx looked thoroughly beaten. As we learned their stories, my parents were grateful that we left Cambodia when we did.

The new arrivals recounted horror stories of torture, starvation, labor camps, murder, and mass killing. All of them had witnessed death in the worst possible ways. Under the Khmer Rouge, their freedom was denied, and they were to be destroyed if they didn't carry on the work of Angka, the Organization.

We couldn't conceive what they had been through, but their corpse-like appearances told us that they had suffered terribly. As their stories circulated throughout the camp, people panicked, and this ignited the final dispersal of people to a third country. It was a rude awakening for many, including my father, who had hopes that we could return home.

The horror stories of the new refugees also changed the mood inside the camp. Within days, things rapidly deteriorated as people's morale sank. People despaired, became impatient, lost hope. Every week it became common to hear news of rape, incest, adultery, and theft. This was the life of the camp before we left. There was no set method for handling the different crimes taking place. To make matters worse, corruption flourished between the Thai guards and the refugees. Without bribes paid to the guards, it became difficult to get things done.

The bad news continued. We learned that my auntie died. She was my mother's sister who had stayed behind in Cambodia to look after their father. Her two teenage daughters still lived, but her husband had died the year earlier, by what cause we didn't know. Moreover, my grandfather had died of illness a year after our escape. It had been almost four years since we left Cambodia, and the scale of death expanded. Every family in the camp had lost loved ones.

The horror stories of the latest refugees and the unsafe living conditions in the camp made my father see the hopelessness of our situation. With the camp no longer a safe haven, he decided it was time for us to move on. As displaced people living in a refugee camp, we were qualified to go to other countries, such as the United States, Canada, France, England, and Switzerland. Everyone abandoned their thoughts of returning to Cambodia, and waves of people emigrated to any country that would grant them asylum.

Although Dad's younger brother left for Canada the previous year, our family decided to seek asylum in the States, along with the majority of relatives submitting paperwork at that time. Churches sponsored most Cambodian refugees, but no such sponsorships were available at the time we were ready to emigrate. Ultimately, my family was sponsored by one of my mother's sisters who had already emigrated to Dallas, Texas.

Once our refugee applications were submitted, everything happened fast. Six months later our family relocated to another camp in Bataan, Philippines. This was the final stage before we would be granted resettlement in the United States.

I clearly remember the day we departed from Aranyaprathet in the fall of 1979. It was a hot morning and for me a day of mixed emotions. My mother walked me to the school, so I could say good-bye to my teacher. The Thai flag flew peacefully above the school grounds. As we approached my teacher, I could see my classmates lined up and waiting to enter the building. Mom signaled for me to *noop*, a gesture of respect for which I placed my palms together in front of me and bowed. Even though I was happy to leave the camp, it tore me up inside to leave school and the teacher with whom I felt bonded. As the teacher lightly touched my left shoulder, I nearly burst into tears. I lowered my head to hide my face and quickly turned. As I walked away, the tears gushed. Behind me, Mom murmured, *"Karp chai*(Thank you)," to the teacher before she followed after me. I didn't look back once. That was the parting scene from my first school.

Mom and I joined the rest of our family in the area where we were told to meet for the departure. Four buses were parked in the front of the camp waiting to transport us. Aside from the people who were leaving, many other people stood around. Some were spectators, but many were relatives saying good-bye. Soon, one by one, each family's name was called. We loaded our belongings into the cargo hold of the bus and boarded. Inside the bus it was very noisy. Toddlers cried. Young kids ran up and down the aisle. Excited, the adults chatted loudly. The bus engine hummed endlessly in the background. For my mother and I, it was neither a happy nor a sad moment.

"I don't know why some people are so happy," she said aloud. "For all we know, this bus could be taking us back to Cambodia." A born skeptic, she stared suspiciously at the officials.

A few other people agreed with her. There had been rumors that refugees from another camp were packed onto a bus and unloaded somewhere in Cambodia some months prior. She was worried that this would happen to us. Our destinies were in the hands of the people in charge of the buses. As our bus slowly drove away from the camp, my mother's suspicions gave me the chills.

Hours later, though, we arrived at our destination, a port from which we would take a ship to the Philippines. I couldn't take my eyes off a gigantic black building that towered over all the small shops along the shore. I had never seen anything so big, and I marveled at the size of it though not its appearance. It was nothing but black steel with no windows. As I was thinking to myself that this is what you call a tall building, I heard someone say that it was a ship, our ship.

I wanted to shout hallelujah out of pure joy. I was happy about the grand adventure and relieved we would not be sent back to Cambodia. *A big ship like this doesn't go to Cambodia*, I told myself.

Mom was no longer annoyed by the noise and excitement around her, and with my spirits lifted, suddenly everything became colorful. I noticed the girls my age traveling with us who wore bright dresses with layers and layers of ruffles. After so many years of drab clothes, the colorful dresses seemed abnormal. Even though I had on my everyday clothes—a faded sarong, a shirt that had once been white but was now gray, and flip-flops—I felt the colors in me, and it brought a smile to my lips.

My father noticed the colorful dresses on the other girls too. I thought about asking him to buy me a dress that matched my mood. Sure enough, minutes later Dad and I were at a nearby stall that was selling the extra fluffy dresses. Together we stood back, heads tilted to one side, surveying all of the ones hung on display. Except for the different colors, they all looked the same.

"It seems like it would get in the way," my ever-practical Dad finally said.

I didn't make a fuss. I was a timid little girl, and a fancy dress would draw too many eyes to me. I would have wound up wanting to hide in between the ruffles.

We went back to join the others in line. Soon our names were called, and we hurried aboard the ship. The inside of the ship was maybe the size of a high school gym and completely bare: no beds. Each family was assigned a small space barely large enough for everyone to sleep. People had to walk over each other to get around, as there was no room for aisles between the rows of people. While Mom and Dad busied themselves with the setup of our little area, my siblings and I explored the ship. We discovered that the other part of it was like a maze. Many of the doors were locked and had red signs marked with an X, but somehow we managed to find the bathroom.

We found our way to some stairs that led to the huge deck, where a crowd had gathered for a last look at the shore of Thailand. There was an atmosphere of euphoria. As the ship slowly sailed from the port, I stood in a kind of trance. The landscape facing me became fuzzy. Holding on to the railing, I told myself, *This is it*. A warm breeze roused me from my thoughts, and I felt a sense of relief, as if the breeze had taken away my worries, like I had just been blessed with holy water.

Bataan, The Philippines

It took five days for the ship to reach the Philippines, and the voyage did not bring the adventure I had expected. I was terribly seasick by the second day and couldn't eat anything. For four days I lay on the metal floor wishing my head would stop spinning; every waking minute was torture. I felt the constant crash of the waves against the ship, which only made my insides churn worse. The nausea was unrelenting, and there was no way to steady myself or ease my discomfort. My mother tried to force a little rice and water into me, only to see me vomit minutes later. In fact, it seemed like all I did was retch. By the third day, fatigue took over, and I drifted in and out of sleep, feeling as if I was on my deathbed. I don't remember disembarking from the ship. I was that ill.

During the five days at sea, the only foods provided to the refugees were plain rice and boiled eggs—morning, noon, and night. My father brought along ramen noodles and donuts. That too made my stomach turn like everything in the ship. So much so that it took five years after this journey before I could eat ramen noodles, ten years before I could eat donuts, and thirty years before I could stomach boiled eggs. The smell of these foods never fails to trigger flashbacks of being on that ship.

Years later I learned that because so many of the refugees on our ship were seasick, none were transported to the Philippines by boat thereafter. We were the only group who went through that ordeal.

* * *

When we arrived at the camp in the Philippines, we reunited with our relatives who had been transported there by air. They welcomed us with food: *pla dak, pla too*, and rice. *Pla dak* and *pla too* are essentially rotten fish, something none too palatable to *falang* but a delicacy for us.

Pla dak consists of preserved raw fish that is used as a flavor enhancer for cooking but also as a dipping sauce when all kinds of herbs are added to it. *Pla too* is cooked and preserved sardines that can be eaten with rice. It too is often mashed up and mixed with spices to become a dipping sauce for vegetables. I like it best when it's fried with garlic.

In the camp in Thailand, people joked about saying good-bye to *pla too*, because it was considered a poor man's food. It was cheap, and we consumed so much of it. "May you never have to eat *pla too* again" was a common farewell said to those who were emigrating to the West.

As a kid I didn't mind *pla too*, but I was not a fan of *pla dak*. The thought of eating a rotten raw fish that had been sitting in a jar for months made me turn my nose the other way. During the five days at sea, however, I remember missing *pla dak* and *pla too* equally.

When our relatives greeted us in the camp, we were probably happier to see the food than them. My mouth watered at the smell of fried *pla too*, lime, fresh cut chilies, and an assortment of herbs. For the very first time in my life, the aroma of these combined ingredients revived my appetite. When everyone settled down to a meal that day, I followed suit, dipping a piece of crispy fried *pla too* into the *pla dak* sauce and placing it atop my plate of warm jasmine rice. With my hand I scooped the food into my mouth. Right away my strength returned, and we all exclaimed that this was the best meal ever.

As with the camp in Thailand, we were among the first wave of refugees to stay on Bataan Islands. Unlike the Thai camp, we were free to roam the area, and it seemed fairly safe. Bataan was filled with untouched forest, which was a lifesaver. My father and the other men immediately set out to go hunting and discovered that game was plentiful, and that all kinds of familiar plants and vegetables could be foraged. Birds, fish, and wild animals were easily caught. In no time, Mom dried and preserved all sorts of meats. Dad brought some seeds from Thailand, and within a month his garden had all kinds of herbs. Since the climate was the same as Thailand and Cambodia, my father's garden was happy.

International aid organizations gave us rations too, but the food was not to our liking. Luckily, a market soon sprang up and once again all kinds of food became available. In this camp, which also had refugees from Vietnam and Laos, the market offered even more variety than the one in Thailand.

For a few months, my father and Uncle Lee found a worthwhile way to earn a little money. They harvested a special vine that could be easily woven into baskets. For two months they devoted themselves to weaving colorful baskets of all shapes and sizes day and night. Baskets hung from wall to wall in our tiny living space. Big, small, plain, fancy—I liked them all. Many people, including refugees and aid workers, bought them for practical uses or as souvenirs.

Although the baskets were an attraction, our resident monkey was perhaps the bigger draw. One day when he was in the forest, my father discovered the monkey in one of his traps. The monkey limped because one of its legs had been injured by the trap.

"But why did you bring the monkey home?" I asked Dad as soon as I laid my eyes on the curious creature.

"I couldn't leave an injured monkey in the forest," he said.

After a month the monkey recovered and ran wild in our hut. Uncontrollable, it threw things at people, and I was terrified of the naughty little creature. I was relieved when one of the aid workers bought the monkey from us.

As for my father and uncle's newfound hobby, it only lasted about six months before other people began weaving baskets as well, and the vines became harder to find. The forest that surrounded us had been pristine when we arrived, but with a camp full of people nearby, it didn't remain that way for long.

* * *

During our first week in Bataan, we were told there was a river about twenty minutes from the camp. This river became a weekly getaway for us kids. The walk to it was as pleasant as the river itself. Evergreens growing thick above the path cooled us with their shade. We nibbled the wild berries that grew among the flowers of glorious colors along the way. We could hear the calls of wild animals in all directions. Monkeys dashed back and forth with excitement as soon as they spotted us. Unlike the bare and desert-like camp in Thailand, this one was a pleasant change.

As lovely as it was to be able to wander off and play in the river, the camp in the Philippines had a dark side to it. There was intense animosity between the Cambodian, Vietnamese, and Lao people, the result of a long history of border conflicts between neighboring countries. Despite the wars that displaced them, the refugees remained patriotic, especially during soccer games where insults traded on the playing field were a common sight. I recall seeing one fight that involved a large crowd, fists, and men wielding sticks. The women—mothers, wives, and sisters—stepped in and settled the angry men.

After a few of these fights, unless you were an aid worker, you didn't venture out of your territory for fear of being harassed or beat up. The camp was set up to have three territories: one each for Cambodians, Lao, and Vietnamese. My parents were adamant that my siblings and I stay out of trouble. I never ventured beyond Cambodian turf except to go to the market, which remained safe despite all the territorial conflicts.

Life in either refugee camp, Thailand or the Philippines, had its dangers and difficulties, but I dreaded the toilets in the Bataan camp the most, bar none. In Thailand, the open fields served as our toilets —find a bush and do your business. Done. In Bataan there was an attempt to have a proper camp bathroom. Except it wasn't a flush toilet, but a long thin tunnel that didn't flow properly. The stench and the flies were so unbearable that I resorted to the old means of going in the bushes.

I was sure that America had better toilets, and I was right, because before we left the Philippines, an aid worker trained us at length about Western bathrooms. I remember looking over my mother's shoulder as she flipped through pictures of white, shiny toilets. Like everyone, I was fascinated by them as well as nervous—I would have to remember to sit and not squat! Of this, I made a mental note.

Sisters: Me, Lai, and Let.

My grandmother, V Chalermchai. This photo was taken
in the early 1980s.

Left to right: Uncle Lee, Uncle Aun, and my dad.

From Left to Right: Sang, Me, Ong, Bangoun, Uncle Lee sitting on the steps.

My father, Butsy Bunla.

My mother, Toeur Bunla.

The house I was born in. This photo was taken in 2012.

After Mom passed away in 2010,
Dad became a monk and remained a
monk until his death in 2012.

Encounters

"Who are those ladies?" I asked my mother the first time I saw nuns at the camp in Bataan.

"They are good people," she replied.

About once a week the nuns came to the camp and handed us a fancy magazine with photos of what seemed like paradise. Up until then the only religion I knew was Buddhism. I didn't understand what or who God was. During one whole week in April, there were more nuns around than usual to celebrate Christ's crucifixion with the refugees. Our family didn't participate in any of the events. However, on the last night, they showed a movie outdoors, and that was something I didn't want to skip. I begged Mom to let me see it, and she agreed that I could but not with the crowd. She let me watch it from the front of our shack. I was too far away to hear the sound, which didn't matter anyway. The movie was in English, a language I didn't understand. So I didn't throw a fit about wanting to get closer.

Halfway through the movie came a scene of a man hanging on a cross and oozing blood. Shocked, I yelled for my mother and dashed inside our shack, blinking to erase the scene now stuck in my head. I parked myself next to Mom without saying a word. The last time I felt such fear was at the farmhouse in Thailand when I constantly fretted that the Khmer Rouge would take away the people I love one by one, and I had no control over it. That night that fear returned. I cuddled extra close to my mother and couldn't sleep soundly unless she was turned to my side. I pulled her arms across to cover me like a blanket. Whenever she shifted so that her back was to me, I tossed and turned while trying to get the Khmer Rouge out of my head. At one point that night, I became convinced that we could never escape the Khmer Rouge entirely, that the Khmer Rouge killing sprees were as inevitable as the death of Christ in the movie and as unstoppable as a force of nature. This filled me with a sense of defeat. For weeks thereafter I was consumed by my ignited fears of the Khmer Rouge and death and losing more relatives. I didn't know how to talk about my fears. When the need to feel a little safer overwhelmed me, I curled up next to Mom.

* * *

It was in the Philippines camp that I first encountered *falang* kids my age. One hot, sunny Monday afternoon, I noticed a group of kids approaching from a distance as I was alone in the garden picking herbs for Mom. I stopped and squinted for a better look. Adults and some of my friends peered out from their huts. This was the first time any of us had ever seen *falang* kids, and we were curious about them. We stared at them, and they at us as time seemed to stand still. I was in awe of their porcelain skin, blond hair, and blue eyes. They even smelled sweet, like the fruity gum they chewed. I would do anything to look like them and be like them. I made a note to myself to beg my father to buy me some of that bubble gum.

However, after a minute the sound of the *falang* children popping their bubble gum changed my mood. Instead of wonder I felt resentment and agitated by the way they stared at me. I didn't like being pitied—by them or anyone. I had felt the same when a *falang* man took photographs of the refugee children in the camp in Thailand. The other children were so eager to have their picture taken that they hurled themselves at him, shouting, "Me! Me! Me!" I watched him from afar, amused until he turned the camera directly at me. I tried to move out of the way, but the camera moved with me. The other children rushed over and hovered over me, because they wanted their pictures taken. It was all fun and games to them, but the photographer distracted them from me. As soon as that was done, he pointed his camera at me again. As I was about to move off, he gestured for me to stay put. Confused, I stood still for a moment, at first flattered that he wanted to take pictures of me. But then a little voice inside me spoke, *Don't pity me.* I ducked out of the way, the man's camera still snapping pictures.

The *falang* children who stared and pointed at us as they popped their gum conjured the same irritation. We were around the same age yet worlds apart. They looked so clean and beautiful, right down to their shoes, dresses, and hairpins. I resented them for all that they had.

After the young spectators left, the adults commented about their beauty.

"They had gorgeous white skin!"

"They were all beautiful."

"They all seemed so smart."

I quietly left the scene feeling like I didn't exist, wishing I could vanish.

The Big Move

After seven months in Bataan, my father announced that we were on the list to go to America. He grinned. I grinned too and spent the rest of the day drifting through dream after dream about America. I didn't care where Dallas, Texas, was, as long as it was in the United States of America. I skipped down the road, smiling, waving, and chattering to strangers.

A month later my family and other refugees once again boarded a bus that would take us to the airport, our excitement riding high. Along the way we passed thatched roof houses here and there. A few hours into the trip, the bus stopped for a bathroom break in a small city. Local people swarmed the bus trying to sell us goods through the windows.

My family ignored the peddlers and ate a lunch that Mom prepared inside the bus, our usual delicious travel food of sticky rice, dried meats, and a dipping sauce. As the bus resumed the long journey, I began to be queasy with motion sickness. Mom gave me Dramamine, which knocked me out, so much so I slept through the bus ride. When I woke up, I was on the plane. I finally opened my eyes at the sound of my stomach growling. A craving for warm jasmine rice with *tom yum* soup and fried *pla too* filled me. The food on the plane didn't look or smell familiar, let alone as good as the food I craved, but I did catch a whiff of something that reminded me of a sweet dish made from black beans, tapioca, condensed milk, and coconut milk. I was ecstatic and put a huge spoonful in my mouth. Right away, eyes bulging, I was horrified by the taste.

I looked over at Mom and mumbled, with my mouth still full, "Ugh! What is this?" I couldn't help but spit out the horrible stuff, making a bit of a mess, and pushing the plate away from me.

"Next time don't take such a big bite, especially when you don't know what it is you're eating," Mom scolded me as she helped me clean up. For the rest of the trip, I didn't eat anything and ignored the hunger pangs that sometimes woke me up.

PART III
STARTING OVER

California

I was still asleep when our plane landed in San Francisco. I didn't wake up until a few hours later when we had been transported to the Presidio military base nearby.

"Where are we?" I asked Mom, groggy and rubbing crust from my eyes.

"We're in America, at a military housing facility."

"What happened to the plane?"

"We landed a few hours ago."

"How come I didn't know about it?" I cried.

"Mom went a little crazy with the Dramamine," someone said.

I wanted so much to see the fancy airport that I'd heard about in the Philippines. Cranky and disappointed, I scowled.

"Remember the boat ride?" my mother said. "Did you want to relive that?"

Everyone on our plane to San Francisco was a refugee, and all of us were taken to the military base to recuperate before the last leg of our journey: our final destinations in the United States. In two days time, our family was to board a plane to Texas.

At the temporary facility, we were shown to our room and the bathroom. *Sit not squat*, I reminded myself while the social workers did a toilet demonstration at a communal bathroom. Later that day it seemed as though everything we were taught flew straight from our heads, because I could smell the bathroom down the hall. I groaned at the thought of another smelly camp bathroom. Eventually I had to go, as much as I dreaded it.

Sure enough, when I went into the bathroom, I was disappointed to find that all the toilets were filthy. I saw shoes prints on the seats, and none of them were flushed. I had to go so badly that I had no choice. Once done, I searched for the knob or a handle or whatever it was that had been shown to me earlier that day. For the life of me, I couldn't find it. I broke out into a sweat and ran out of the bathroom for a breath of fresh air before dashing back to try once more. After three failed attempts, I left the unflushed toilet to look for Lai to help me. As always she was with Let, and they both acted like they didn't hear me. I stood over them and talked nonsense to annoy them. Finally Lai got up, huffing and puffing, and followed me to the bathroom.

Minutes later we stood over a toilet and began pulling, pushing, and beating on everything we could get our hands on. I went to another toilet so I was not in Lai's way. All of a sudden, a loud noise shocked both of us. We backed away, looked at each other, and raced out of the bathroom, stopping just outside the door. Lai panted heavily, while I scanned the hallway to make sure no one saw us.

"What did you do?" I accused Lai.

"I don't know. I must have pushed something," she said.

"I hope you didn't break anything in there. It sounds broken."

We looked at each other, not knowing what to do. When the sound stopped, we peeked into the bathroom again.

Seeing nothing unusual, Lai pulled my shirt and said, "Come on."

I followed her a few steps inside, shadowing her every move. When she bent over, I bent over, even if I had no idea what we were looking for.

When we made it to the toilet I had used, Lai exclaimed, "It's clean! I did it," raising her hands in the air like she'd won a prize.

"Here, this is the handle I pushed," she said as she showed me.

She pushed it again, and the water spun and twirled in a whirlpool. The noise of it made me move closer to Lai who was still overcome by the spirit. We flushed every toilet in the women's bathroom that day and the days that followed.

* * *

"Mr. Bunla, you have a visitor," a social worker told Dad the next morning while we sat around, bored.

Surprised, Dad looked over at Mom before cautiously following the social worker to the office. Ten minutes later Dad came back but not alone. There was an older man with him; both of them had smiles.

My mother yelled, "*Lung!* (Uncle!)" She ran to greet him and then placed her palms together and bowed to show him respect. The rest of us followed her and did the same. This was one of my great uncles, although I had never met him before. His mother was a sister of my grandmother, and prior to the war, his family lived in another village.

"Come, please sit," Mom insisted.

"We had no idea that you escaped Cambodia. When the Khmer Rouge took over, there was no way to reach you," Dad said to him.

"Yes, my whole family managed to escape, but we had no idea about your family," Uncle said. "We still don't know the whereabouts of all the others. When I heard that your family made it here, I had to see you."

My parents and my uncle talked for hours that day. I sat there quietly, taking all of it in. Every now and then one of them would lower their heads in sorrow, shaking their heads in disbelief about some sad bit of news.

Great Uncle learned of our arrival from the cousin of my friend Sang, who had traveled with us on the plane. Sang's family did not go to the military base, because they had been picked up at the airport by their cousin who lived across the street from Great Uncle in West Oakland, California.

"You must stay here in California," he said to Dad. "Come stay at my house. There's room, and we can look for a place for your family in the neighborhood. We have a community that will help you."

My father agreed. The immigration office granted permission for our family to stay in California. The following day Great Uncle came for us with two cars. Because there was no room, Let, Lai, and I were stuffed into the trunk of a Volkswagen hatchback. I hated that ride because at high speed I faced the road behind us rather than in front of us. I leaned back to steady myself. All I could see was the ceiling of the car and clear blue sky to the side. Halfway home I caught sight of a bridge that made me sit up to get a better view. It was the Bay Bridge. I couldn't wrap my head around something that grand. It welcomed me, and so to me the Bay Bridge was my Statue of Liberty.

As we drove through the streets of what would be my neighborhood, to my surprise I saw black kids everywhere—on the street, on the front porches, in the park. I had thought that America only had white people. At least that was the understanding that had circulated in the refugee camps. I wondered if we had actually come to the US and not some other country.

"Mom, there are black people here," I said to her. She laughed uneasily and looked to my great uncle for help.

"You will not see any white people in this part of town, *lug* (daughter). There are only black and Asian people living here," he said.

It was all very confusing. I didn't know what to think next.

* * *

I saw Sang the next day while sitting outside Great Uncle's house with Lai. We exchanged a few words about my great uncle, and she introduced me to her cousin Bangoun. Bangoun and I exchanged shy smiles. Although we got off to a quiet start, for the next few years, Sang, Bangoun, and I were inseparable. Sang was studious and sexy. Bangoun was the youngest and had a charming smile that could win over any boy. We were like *Charlie's Angels*. There was no doubt as to which Angel I resembled. I was Kate Jackson, Sang was Farrah Fawcett, and Bangoun was Jaclyn Smith. They were my childhood friends.

During my first summer in America, the summer of 1980, Sang, Bangoun, and I roamed the streets of West Oakland, picking berries in abandoned lots and stealing plums from the neighbor's yard. Bangoun, who had lived in America for a year by then, explained that most Americans didn't pick the fruit from their trees to eat but planted them to be ornamental. I thought this was a terrible waste.

With a year's experience under her belt, Bangoun educated Sang and me about American ways. Anyone who knew better would not have ventured into the areas we wandered, but we were all naïve, including Bangoun.

"Why is that man sleeping on the street? Is he all right?" I asked her about a man who looked dead.

"Oh, he's homeless," Bangoun said.

My head spun. "Isn't this America? The place where money falls from the sky? The land of opportunity?"

"Just ignore him, and we should be all right," Bangoun advised.

As we passed strangers, sometimes one would talk to us, but many simply ignored us. One time a man said something to us, and being a positive person, Sang interpreted his comment as, "I think he just said hello."

"He said *fuck you*," Bangoun corrected. We huddled and laughed so hard at Sang's translation that we forgot about being insulted.

* * *

Our area of West Oakland was home to many refugees, mostly Hmong, but also Lao and Cambodian. My great uncle lived in a three-bedroom house on a quiet street with his wife, his youngest daughter, and his older daughter and her husband. For almost a month, my family of seven occupied every inch of their living room. It was crowded but comfortable, and great uncle's family never made us feel unwelcome. "This is like your house. Please make yourself at home," Great Uncle told us time and time again.

When he was drunk, which was often, Great Uncle rambled on about this and that, and we found him very entertaining. Even Lai, who could never hold her tongue, and Mom, who was critical, never uttered a bad word about him.

A few weeks later, my family moved into a one-bedroom apartment around the corner from Great Uncle. That was all we could afford. With seven of us there was no privacy at all. We constantly got in each other's way and had to time everything carefully to make the living situation work. The only bedroom was jam-packed with two queen beds that Dad, Mom, Let, Lai, and I slept on, packed in like sardines. In the living room, there were two sofas and a twin bed. Uncle Lee slept in the bed, while Ath had the sofa bed. The apartment was tight, but our family was fine with that since we were used to living in small spaces. Besides, we were just grateful to have an apartment of our own.

I spent the next eight years of my life in that apartment, including two years of elementary school, two years of junior high, and four years of high school. Let, Lai, Ath, and Uncle Lee moved away as soon as they were married. Dad and Mom lived there the longest, ten years.

* * *

In the camps in Thailand and the Philippines, I dreamed of being in a real school, making friends, and learning English. I could hardly contain my excitement. *This is it,* I told myself on my first day of school. That morning the other refugee kids and I walked the five blocks to Prescott

Elementary School. Although Sang, Bangoun, and I went to Prescott, we were all in separate classes. I was placed in the third grade with the rest of the eleven- and twelve-year-olds.

My first day of class truly captured the meaning of being a stranger in a strange land. Not one thing was familiar. The walls were covered with colorful artwork, and the smell of glue and crayons permeated the room. All the other kids in the classroom seemed to be having a contest as to who could talk the loudest. When my teacher, Mrs. Scott, could get a word in, she spoke fast, like a thousand words per minute. She rambled on about something for such a long time that dots of spit collected at the corners of her mouth.

At midmorning on my second day of school, Mrs. Scott handed me a sheet of paper, spoke fast to me again, and pointed toward the door. To this day, I have no idea what the paper said. I assumed that she wanted me to go home, so that is what I did. On the way home, I was so caught up in my worries that I became lost. I was eleven years old, spoke no English, and couldn't find my way around the worst part of Oakland! I retraced my steps back to school and started again. This time I made it home, and once there I couldn't wait to hide in the bathroom and cry.

"Why are you home early?" my mother asked.

I shrugged and walked away. My parents left me alone, and I was thankful for that. For the rest of the day, I nursed my badly bruised spirit. I kept to myself, moped around the house, and sometimes escaped to the bathroom to cry some more. The crying seemed to bring back all the bad memories, including those of Ai Sang Thout. I cried for him, I cried for my dead relatives, and I cried for Kagh.

* * *

The fall of 1980 marked the beginning of my long battle with school and my struggle to adapt to my new life in the States. I had thought everything would be so much easier in the United States, a notion that was hard for me to let go of. In the years that followed, it seemed that with every new experience, no matter how many obstacles I overcame, more followed.

Academically, I did so poorly that I repeated third grade. By the end of that year, my second at Prescott, a translator met with my parents and me to explain that I would go to junior high the next year.

"Why?" Dad asked.

"Because she is too old to remain in elementary school," the translator said.

My heart sank when I saw the disappointment on my parents' faces. I was promoted because of my age, not because I was smart.

Although technically a third grader, I rehearsed the graduation ceremony with the sixth-graders. As we marched and sang, my mind drifted elsewhere. When we practiced the song "The Greatest Love Of All" by Whitney Huston, I wanted to gag, because I didn't believe that my future would be any better.

On graduation day the room filled with proud parents, but no one from my family came to the ceremony. I had given my parents the invitation, but since they couldn't read it, they didn't understand what it meant. I did what we had rehearsed for the ceremony, including the "step-step-clap" dance to "Ebony and Ivory," but in my head I was thinking that this better be the last time I had to sing that song. When the names of the other students were called to receive their promotion certificates, people in the audience whistled and cheered so much I got a headache. When my name was called, there was a pause in the noise, then a hesitant clap, followed by another hesitant clap. When the announcer realized the awkwardness of the moment, she quickly announced the next name to restore the happy atmosphere. The whistles and cheers picked up again as I marched from that stage feeling like shit. I wished that I could magically transport myself out of there. That was my parting thought about my graduation ceremony.

When I got home, I sank on the sofa with relief.

"What's this paper?" my mother asked.

"My certificate of promotion."

"How come you didn't tell me it was today?"

"It's no big deal," I said and went to look for snacks.

My parents didn't get upset with me for not telling them about the ceremony, which made me happy. In fact, the matter was never brought up again. That was fine by me.

* * *

The summer before junior high I spent half of each day attending summer school and the other half watching television. School didn't make much of an impression on me, except that all of the students were Asian, and that we were all bused to a school in East Oakland.

For the most part, summer school was a waste of time. The only upside to it was that the Charlie's Angels were together. The downside, as if I needed one, was that the bus ride gave me motion sickness. I would have gotten out of summer school if I could. When I asked my mother if it was necessary, she replied, "Everyone else is doing it." There was no arguing with that. During those early years in the States, the general rule was that if the majority of the people in the community were doing something, then chances are I would have to do it also.

That summer I learned more from watching TV and listening to music than anything else.

"I'm going to break that TV," Dad threatened many times when the sound of the television woke him up from his afternoon nap. That was my cue to duck out to Auntie's house, the next one over, and resume my TV consumption from there.

When I wasn't watching TV, I was glued to the radio. The Saturday morning shows had the best and latest songs, and I stayed in bed to listen to them. Not even the Charlie's Angels could persuade me to miss out on my music. I got out of bed only when one of my parents complained about my laziness.

I loved music so much that I stole my Dad's cassette recorder to make tapes of my favorite songs. I spent hours playing those songs over and over until I could write all the words down on paper. It never took long for Dad to notice his cassette tape was missing. When he asked everyone about it, I shrugged as if innocent and left the house to search for the Charlie's Angels. Mom mumbled something to Dad about old age and memory loss.

A week later Dad found the cassette he was looking for, but instead of Cambodian songs he heard "Staying Alive" by my favorite group, The Bee Gees.

"Mai!" he yelled in a way that made my hair stand on end.

"Uh oh…I'd better go," I told the Charlie's Angels. When I entered the bedroom, Dad held the cassette in my face.

"I'm so sorry. I promise to never do it again," I pleaded.

Mom came to my rescue. (How I love her!) "You barely listen to that cassette anyway," she said to Dad.

As I backed out of the room and ran to Auntie's house, Dad shouted, "She should know better."

I don't know how long they argued since I stayed away, had dinner with Auntie's family, and only returned home when I knew Dad would be asleep. I crawled into bed between Mom and Lai, a space removed from Dad, and went to sleep praying that he would forget about it the following day.

* * *

The fall semester of 1982 approached too fast. Whenever I thought about school, I wanted to crawl into a den and stay put for the rest of the year, just like a bear with its annual hibernation. In elementary school I faced language barriers, but in junior high I had to deal with bullies. By then I knew enough English to understand all the insults thrown at me almost daily.

The first time a bully said, "Go back to where you came from, you boat people," I thought to myself, *How on earth did he know that I was on a boat from Thailand to the Philippines?*

A few months later in a history class, I learned about the term "boat people" as the bully knew it. It generally referred to Vietnamese refugees risking their lives to escape their war-torn country in small boats.

That ignorant asshole, I muttered to myself. That particular bully often picked on me and the other refugee students. But no matter how much I cursed the bullies—there were a few of them—their words still hurt, and the hurt ate me up inside.

I did anything and everything to avoid the kids who were most likely to pick on the refugee kids. For instance, I knew which areas and which streets to avoid in order to get home without being harassed.

One day I came home and threw myself onto the sofa, huffing and puffing so loud that Mom asked, "What's wrong with you?"

I contemplated what I should say to my un-American mom who grew up in a completely different environment and decided to say nothing. I didn't tell her that other kids called me a Chinaman, made fun of my native language, made fun of the way I talked, and told me that I stank and didn't belong in America.

By the end of junior high, the bullies succeeded in making me feel ashamed to be me. I was so tired of it all, and I craved for a more peaceful and normal existence, for better times. Nonetheless, in the back of my mind, I knew I'd rather deal with life as it was than have to live in a refugee camp or worse—to be in Cambodia where the Khmer Rouge was still in control.

* * *

Except for math and physical education, all my other junior high classes were English as a Second Language (ESL). One of my ESL teachers, Mr.

Haseman, also taught geography while the other teacher, Mr. Noodle, also taught Spanish. Mr. Noodle was an African American hippie. For an entire semester in eighth grade, Mr. Noodle made the class sing "Happy Hanukkah" every day!

I knew what was coming when he skipped over to a piano, parked himself on the bench, and announced, "OK, class! I want to hear you sing like you've got the spirit in you. Clap your hands and sing your hearts out!" Those sitting in the first few rows learned to dodge the spittle that sprayed everywhere when he talked.

I asked myself, *How on earth am I going to learn English singing this song?* When we weren't singing, we were split into groups of three or four and given English worksheets to complete. That was the extent of our classroom activities. After a while I became bored with both the singing and the worksheets. The one good thing that came out of the class with Mr. Noodle was my best friend, Lany Gonzales. Lany and her sisters had just immigrated from the Philippines and joined their mother who had been living in Oakland. Lany spoke English better than the rest of us, so she only had to take ESL classes for one semester. I, on the other hand, continued to live and breathe ESL.

Although my geography class with Mr. Haseman was also an ESL class, I found myself looking forward to it. At first I thought that was because it was the last period of the school day, but soon I realized that it was Mr. Haseman who made geography so much fun. He engaged us rather than just leaving us to do worksheets like the others. All of the students respected him and enjoyed his teaching style. It didn't hurt either that Mr. Haseman looked a lot like Gregory Peck in the movie, *Roman Holiday*.

Halfway through the first semester I discovered that Mr. Haseman was a Vietnam veteran. I liked him even more for that, because it clearly helped him relate with the refugee students from Southeast Asia. When I teased him about how the Uncle Ben's rice eaten by Americans tasted horrible, his comeback was that he only ate jasmine rice, the kind made by his Vietnamese wife. That Mr. Haseman had a wife from Vietnam gave me yet another reason to like him.

When I finished junior high and entered high school, I was determined to be done with ESL classes, but I didn't get my way. This time my ESL teacher, Mr. Thomas, also taught mechanics, which made no sense to me. Who on earth appointed a mechanics teacher to teach English to students struggling with their English?

On the first day of class, Mr. Thomas, dressed in gray overalls, introduced himself and gave us a few instructions. My desk was next to a door that led to a workshop filled with all sorts of car parts waiting to be put together. Each time the door swung open, the smell of gasoline and rusty metal seeped into the room, which caused me constant headaches. I can honestly say that Mr. Thomas didn't teach us a thing. In fact, after the roll was called, he escaped to his workshop where he worked on the cars, leaving us on our own for the whole period.

Cultural Collisions

Every day I grumbled about how my ESL classes were a waste of time, but I didn't complain to anyone because that would upset my parents. Still, it seemed to me that no one cared about giving an education to a bunch of refugee students from a poor neighborhood. I knew I couldn't fight the way things were, but I had to find a way out. That's when I decided to get involved with sports. This news did not go down well with Dad and Mom though.

"You'll learn nothing. It serves no purpose," Dad fumed. "Young ladies don't play sports!"

My parents took turns imploring me to not do it. "What will our friends think?" they yelled as I rushed out of the room with my hands over my ears.

Sports brought to light the wide differences in our generations. The Asian community that we lived in met my parents' needs, but it didn't meet mine. Since they didn't work, my parents hardly ventured outside the Asian community. They had no need to, except to go to places such as the doctor's office or the welfare department. They also never got involved in any activity that was not Asian. Whenever they weren't sure about something, my parents always resorted to saying, "Let's do it the way we did it back in the village."

I wasn't the only kid my age caught in a generation gap dilemma. Like most teenagers, my peers and I wanted to be accepted, wanted to feel like we belonged. Sadly, most of the teenage refugees found the acceptance they craved by joining gangs. Violence and drugs became a part of their daily lives. It was no surprise that young girls, some as young as fifteen, became pregnant. The mores of our culture said we shouldn't date, let alone have a baby out of wedlock. As a result many girls were pressured to marry young. These marriages were not officiated by the state of California, but they were official in the eyes of the community. Without education or skills, most young couples in this predicament resorted to government assistance and lived in subsidized housing. This was the life for them, and sadly our community approved.

It frightened me to think that I might wind up in a similar situation, so I decided that there was no way in hell I would have a boyfriend. I knew that if I did, even if I survived the inevitable death threats from my parents, I would wind up with something to regret. Besides, it was hard enough being me as it was. It made no sense to add to my hardships.

Aware of the bad influences all around me, my parents forced me to live by their rules to keep me safe. They expected me to behave like a typical village girl back in Cambodia. I was to go to school, come home, and do household chores. We didn't see eye to eye in so many different ways. Things I considered to be good for me, my parents considered to be taboo, like sports.

"Why can't you just be like other kids?" Dad asked when I told him I had to stay after school for softball practice.

"I don't know of any girl who plays soccer," Mom said to me, referring to the only sport she knew by name, the one she saw played in Bataan.

"In America I can play any sport I want," I said. Mom rolled her eyes and threw her hands up in the air.

"I know that, Mai, but it just doesn't look good for you," she said. My parents took turns trying to talk me out of sports, and each always circled back to the fact that I was a girl and not a boy. For them there were things that each gender should and shouldn't do. All their preaching about what women could and couldn't do made me bitter about their way of thinking—so much so, that I rebelled by playing more than one sport. Initially, I only wanted to play softball, but at the end of softball season, my coach asked me to join other teams.

"Hey, Little Bitty," she said, using the nickname she and my teammates called me because I was the shortest, "join our basketball team and volleyball team."

This I did without any hesitation. Playing sports meant I stayed after school year-round. Mom and especially Dad voiced their disappointment constantly. To smooth their ruffled feathers, we came to an arrangement with my coach. I could continue to play sports as long as my coach gave me a ride home after practice, especially during the winter. Since I wanted to play, and coach wanted me on the team, we had a deal. Feeling they had no choice, my parents went along with it for the next three years.

"See you tomorrow, Little Bitty," my coach would say when she dropped me off at home. If we had stopped for gas on the way, she would add, "Thanks for pumping the gas." As a way of thanking her for the almost daily rides home, I would pump the gas. For my parents, my return from practice was a reminder that I was going against the cultural grain. They would get short with me and leave the room when I came in.

At fifteen, things were changing for me—some good and some bad. And although school was going well, I noticed that I was no longer the skinny girl who had arrived in the States. Having traded *pla too* with spicy sauce for hamburgers, fries, and sodas, and having discovered the delights of junk food galore, I wore the results on my hips and thighs. I packed on the pounds. Only five feet tall, I wore size six or seven pants. Worse yet, I had no sense of style, unless you consider "blah" to be a style. While the other girls kept with the eighties trends and went through cans and cans of AquaNet hair spray, I didn't own a single one. I never spiked my hair high like the other cool girls my age. Well, I did one time, when Lany's sister, Michelle, refused to let me go to a prom without looking decent. She spiked my bangs to the fashionable height of two inches. After she was done with me, I disappeared into the bathroom. When I reappeared, my bangs were down to one inch. Michelle came after me again with the AquaNet, but I had to tell her to back off.

In addition to being unattractive, I was socially inept when it came to boys, the very opposite from my group of friends: sexy and flirtatious Sang, Bangoun who was beautiful in an innocent way and smart, and stylish Lany who most guys found to be very cute. Compared to them, I was merely an overweight teenager with severe acne.

I was (and still am) one of those people whose friends always said, "Let me put makeup on you." To this day, Sang, and sometimes Bangoun, offer me a makeover. It never fails to take me back to those old times.

* * *

By the midpoint of high school, I possessed a semblance of confidence. I was no longer in ESL classes, and I had friends outside my circle of Asian friends. My social status at school rose too, thanks to sports. I walked with my head a little higher, and someone from the crowd always cheered me on during a game. My parents never attended any of my games, but I was all right with that. After all, not many teens I knew would want to be seen with their parents, and I wasn't any different.

I can honestly say that I survived high school because of my participation in sports. It gave me balance, and it helped me get out from under things that weighed me down. I did better in school and improved my grades. Although my sports teams lost most of our games, I didn't lose anything. I gained so much just by being a part of them.

During my sophomore year, a math teacher introduced me to Upward Bound, an enrichment program designed for young people from low-income families like mine. Although Upward Bound focused mainly on academics, through it I received help that extended beyond that. I enrolled in the Upward Bound program at Mills College in

Oakland, a part of Oakland that was a different world from the one I knew. Unlike my rough neighborhood, the Mills College campus was open, peaceful, and surrounded by pine-covered hills. The dorms and buildings blended in with their natural surroundings, unlike what I had seen on other university campuses. Being there felt more like a camping trip where nature and people blended in the best possible way. To me, it was a place where the sun always shined.

Through Upward Bound I visited other colleges and was exposed to fun things, like Disneyland and skiing. During the summer we lived on campus, and there would be weeklong trips to compete with Upward Bound teams at other colleges in different activities, such as sports or debates. Because of Upward Bound, I made strides academically and reconnected with my best friend from junior high, Lany, who was also enrolled in Upward Bound at Mills. We had lost touch for a while, because we attended different high schools. I also met some great people with whom I remain friends to this day, like Randy, Munir, Scharade, and Kung. Randy was an African American born and raised in the States. Munir was from Yemen, Scharade from Iran, and Kung from China. At the time I didn't think much about the mix of nationalities among my friends, but looking back it hits me how typical it was for the Bay Area.

Without Lany, my six weeks living on campus at Mills College would have been more frightening and bewildering. She kept me entertained, and I survived calculus class because of her. Everyone had his/her own studying technique, but Lany's was odd. As she studied she pulled out strands of hair. By the end of our study period, there would be a pile of her long black hair on the floor. Somehow Lany's study habit rubbed off on me, so that even now I wind up with bald spots when I'm really focused on something.

Even though I struggled with my Upward Bound classes, which stressed me out, they were the very challenge I needed. My regular high school classwork bored me. In the Upward Bound program, though, I was around other students committed to their studies. They were disciplined about their schoolwork and earned good grades. By contrast, I could barely concentrate for more than an hour and was happy just to pass. Still, prior to joining the program I hadn't thought about going to college. Being in a more academic environment such as that of Upward Bound changed my mind, and college became something I wanted to pursue.

By my last year in high school, things were great for me. At school I threw myself into softball, volleyball, and basketball. On Saturdays and during the summer, I threw myself into the Upward Bound program. Although I wasn't a superstar or didn't make the top percentiles in any of my activities or subjects, I was content with the little things that I accomplished.

Within my West Oakland community, though, nothing seemed to likewise inspire the young people and adults around me, which was disheartening. Without having anything better to do, the adults resorted to gambling. Without having any role models to guide them, the young were drawn into gang life.

I was optimistic, but not everyone felt the same way. One time, as Lai and a friend (who was also Nyaw) talked about the future, they decided that they would go as far as junior college.

"After that I would look for work," one of them said while the other nodded in agreement.

"I plan to finish university," I said happily and without hesitation.

"Don't be silly," Lai's friend said with condescension, "our people don't go to university, let alone finish it."

I didn't like the way her comment made me feel or made me second- guess myself. Toward the end of high school, I was tired of hearing such pessimism from my community. From thereon I refused to live such a narrow existence. I believed that there was more to life than that.

This brought me back to my toddler years in Ban Doug Alaan. Even as a young child, I was aware that in Cambodia my family ranked at the bottom of society. We carried the stigma of being farmers and of being part of an ethnic minority. Both served as reasons why we were ranked in the lowest caste. In Cambodia there were no overrides to the caste system except those paid for through bribes. Cambodian civil servants and military personnel wouldn't do anything for the villagers and were never on duty unless first they saw money on the table. This system of bribes allowed them to live like rich folks, and they in turn behaved as if they were above everybody else. This was something I didn't like at all about Cambodians. They made people like the Nyaw feel small.

In our village, the rich people mostly came from the city and rarely interacted with the rest of us. This is why I am thankful to live in the United States where there is no stigma that stems from a caste system, where discrimination is not so rampant, and where social customs don't dictate my friends. Had I still lived in Cambodia, it would be the same as it always was, and one of my Cambodian friends confirmed this years later in Oakland. As a teenager I had a handful of Cambodian friends, the most I'd ever had. I was close to one in particular, Savone, to whom I could confide almost everything.

One day I asked her, "Savone, if we were in Cambodia right now, do you think we would be friends?"

"Nope," she said without hesitation.

After her reply I went silent and felt a bit awkward, although seconds later we continued talking. Savone described her big house with a high gate in Phnom Penh and how many maids it took to care for the property. Her father had been a high-ranking member of the military. They had a car and mingled only with people of their own class. I told her about my family's life as farmers, and described our wagon and cows in a comic way on purpose. Savone was amused by my family's rustic way of living, and I was amused by how snobby, rich Cambodians thought so highly of themselves. Besides, the war had made refugees of rich and poor alike.

Adjustments

The war in Cambodia had lasting consequences for my family, even after we arrived in the US. The effects of having to move from country to country, and the constant turbulence in our lives, had a crippling effect, especially during our first three years in the States. Ill prepared, we struggled to keep our minds intact, and we all suffered privately in our own ways. Although desperately in need of help, we didn't know what sort of help we needed or even if such help existed. Our early days in our new country were marked by confusion, confinement, and frustration. We had fled the struggle to survive in Cambodia and Thailand only to realize that living in America brought its own kind of survival challenges.

My parents and Uncle Lee suffered the transition worse than my siblings and me, but for a while my Uncle Lee perhaps suffered the most. Thinking about Uncle Lee in those early days always makes me sad. During the first couple years in West Oakland, every day he sat on the steps of our apartment watching us kids play. If he wasn't there, he lay on his small bed in a corner of the apartment staring into space with deep despair evident on his face. I rarely stopped playing to talk to him or even look at him, because there was nothing I could do to make it better. His words from long ago, "I had to escape because the

Khmer Rouge was coming for me," stuck in my head. I didn't want to be reminded about the war and everyone who had died. It was better to ignore Uncle Lee, so I did. Still, I believed that people deserved many chances for happiness, and that's what I dearly wanted for Uncle Lee.

A couple years after we moved to West Oakland, I saw Uncle Lee talking to a divorced mother one day outside our apartment. I remember thinking that it was nice to see him doing that, but I didn't draw any conclusions since the woman was our next-door neighbor. However, a week later the woman came to our apartment to ask if Uncle Lee was around. I told her I didn't know but that my mother was in the bedroom. As I asked our neighbor if she wanted me to get her, she left. Her behavior raised my eyebrows, but I dismissed the idea that she was interested in Uncle Lee since she was much younger than him.

In the months that followed, I noticed that Uncle Lee's clothes were neatly pressed, his hair neatly combed in place, and his mood seemed happier.

"I think Uncle Lee and our neighbor like each other," I reported to Bangoun when I noticed the changes.

"His dentures make him seem ten years younger," she said, and we both covered our mouths and giggled. Later that day I confessed my suspicions to my mother, but she brushed me aside like I was a nuisance. To everyone's astonishment, except Bangoun and mine, a few months later Uncle Lee announced to Dad that he wanted to marry the lady next door. Bangoun and I high-fived each other. I was happy that Uncle Lee had found some share of happiness. They were together until Uncle Lee passed away in 1995.

* * *

My father was brought up to be the breadwinner of the family, and in my eyes he more than fulfilled that duty. He was also hardheaded, stubborn, and raised to be the man in charge. Growing up I was a constant source of irritation for him, and by the time I was a teenager, we didn't get along at all. We rarely talked. When we did, inevitably we didn't see eye to eye on something, and the talk turned into a debate. Except he didn't see it as a debate but as backtalk. I grew up hearing Dad go on and on about all the sins I committed.

"You know, Mai, you will have sin talking back to me," he told me many times. Or he frequently reminded me, "I am your father and I know more than you."

When I was younger, I lashed back by banging pots loudly if I was doing the dishes while he lectured me, or to get away from him I slammed the doors shut so hard the whole house shook. As I got older, I tried to be more like my sister Let. Calm and patient, Let would keep her mouth shut or simply leave the room. Being more like Let helped but not always well enough. Sometimes I lapsed back into trying to reason with him.

"Dad, I'm not talking back to you. I'm just telling you what I think," I said calmly before continuing. "Your thinking is not always right."

This only caused him to smack his lips, shake his head, and walk off muttering, "Kids who grow up in America have lost all respect for their elders!"

With time and maturity, I learned to hold my tongue, tough as it was at times, and ignore the negatives to focus on his good intentions.

* * *

There is no word in Nyaw that describes the post-traumatic stress disorder (PTSD) that affected my mother during those early days in the States. In the beginning no one knew what was wrong with her. She barely ate and became very aloof.

"She's sick," Dad would say when we looked to him for an explanation of what ailed her. When this answer didn't seem to be enough, he might add, *"Pee kow,"* which literally means the ghost was inside of her.

While Mom struggled with PTSD, it seemed that all she did was dream of people she knew back in the village. She reported her dreams to whoever that was in the room with her. "So and so was in my dream last night. She helped me carry a bucket of water in the village." Talking aloud to herself, she would murmur, "I wonder what this means? I wonder if she is still alive."

One day when I was alone with her in the room, my mother grabbed me and called me by the name of a cousin who had been a victim of the Khmer Rouge.

"Get me a cabbage. Go! Hurry!" she yelled at me with terror in her eyes. Then she demanded, "Where is the knife?" Stunned and confused, I couldn't move, which upset my mother even more. Her demands got louder. I backed away, frightened but reluctant to leave the room to get help. I debated locking her inside the room, so she couldn't wander into the kitchen and get a knife. Luckily, Dad heard the commotion from the living room and rushed in.

"What is going on?" he asked Mom. He looked at me and then at Mom, thinking one of us would answer. It was as if my mother didn't hear him. Her eyes were locked on mine like she wanted to hypnotize me. I was afraid to look away, although I didn't recognize my mother in those eyes.

This brought me to tears, and I was babbling, not making any sense, but then I managed to say, *"Pee kow."* Immediately Dad reached for Mom's betel nuts and tossed a few pieces into his mouth. He began chanting a mantra, invoking something to come and cure my mother. I ran out of the room, my mother yelling after me amid the chants, "Where are you going? Come back here!"

I took refuge in Auntie's house for the rest of the day, hoping my father's magic would cure her and watching MTV at full blast. I dreaded going home and avoided doing so until it was so late that everyone was asleep. I peeked into the bedroom and breathed a sigh of relief to see that the lights were off. I quietly slid into my usual spot next to Mom's side of the bed. For the first time in my life, sleeping next to Mom that night kept me awake rather than helped me sleep. I prayed that sleeping next to her would feel safe again. My mother remained fragile for several months, but eventually she got better.

* * *

Out of the four of my siblings, Ath had the hardest time adjusting to life in America. Having arrived at age fifteen, his new world was like a whirlpool he didn't know how to escape. He only attended six months of public high school before transferring to a trade school. Eventually he got a job at a glass company through a friend. He quit after a year and went to live with Let who had married and lived in San Luis Obispo, California. Ath then worked in a greenhouse, preparing flowers for shipment.

Several months after he moved, a shiny red Trans Am parked outside our apartment.

"That's mine," Ath said, grinning from ear to ear.

The following year, the red Trans Am was traded in for a brand-new PT cruiser convertible. When I visited Let and him in San Luis Obispo, he took me to shop at a real mall. Until then the only stores I went to were the Salvation Army and Goodwill.

Ath seemed to be living the American dream, or so we thought. The materialistic things he acquired attracted the attention of some newly arrived refugee ladies, one of whom was a fourteen-year-old Cambodian girl who lived next door to my parents. Within months Ath moved back to Oakland and married this young lady. They were never officially married in California, but in the eyes of the Cambodians, the traditional ceremony sealed the marriage between them. Her age didn't bother them at all, and I realized that this was a part of my culture that I didn't like. Instead of being happy for Ath, I cringed at their age difference.

Ath and his wife lived with her family in their small, two-bedroom house next to us. A little over a year later they had a daughter, Marlina. Two years later Adam was born. Ath continued to work at the glass factory. About a year after his son was born, Ath and his wife began to have serious problems. Since our move to the United States, Ath had befriended guys who smoked, drank, and did drugs. That and other problems ended his marriage. His wife left him and took the two kids with her.

"I don't blame her," I said every time someone brought up the subject.

Not long after his wife left, Ath lost his job and moved into Let's basement. Dad bought a ticket for him to move to Texas and live with our cousins, so he could start a new life. There was a job waiting for him. However, in Texas he easily found friends with the same bad habits. Six months later, without consulting Dad or Mom, Ath returned to Oakland.

"What happened? Why are you back in Oakland?" Dad demanded. Ath walked away from Dad without a word of explanation.

I remember one day when Dad's frustrations with Ath flared into madness, and he took a swing at Ath. My fragile mother threw herself into the fray to stop it, and they all got tangled into each other. All I could see were arms throwing punches.

"What good does this do? Are you crazy?" Mom shouted at Dad.

Right before my eyes, the people I loved fought each other to protect each other. The only thing I could do was yell for them to stop it.

Ath freed himself and fled to his sanctuary in Let's basement. Dad stormed to his room, leaving Mom and me in the living room, shocked and puzzled by what had happened. Mom reached for her betel nut container, and quick as lightening she chewed a mouthful to calm her nerves. I wanted to run off myself and escape this crazy family of mine, but I remained with Mom. No words passed between us as I watched her spit out the betel nut juice into a container, again and again, her red-stained saliva sometimes missing the mark and leaving spots on the carpet and the wall. She didn't seem to care that Let might yell at her later. Finally, her body stopped shaking and her breathing returned to normal. I changed into my running clothes, drove myself to San Leandro Marina, and jogged until my body couldn't move another inch.

After this episode, the whole family avoided discussing Ath because it depressed us and caused arguments. Sadly, Ath still lives in Let's basement, unemployed and possessing only the clothes on his back, just like a man who had escaped a war only yesterday.

* * *

Unlike Ath, the winds shifted in a better direction for Let after our move to the States. She let her past remain in the past and focused on her new life in her new country. She was no longer the pale refugee girl with a distended belly. She had long, beautiful jet-black hair, and at school she easily made friends with Lao kids. Unlike Lai and me, Let loved fancy clothes, the flashier the better, and eye-popping red lipstick. Academically she struggled, but she was having too much fun for that to bother her. When she was home, the phone rang constantly, and Dad was not happy about that. For weeks Let jumped to answer the phone every time it rang, since she didn't want Dad to hear it. Lai and I suspected that Let had a boyfriend. We later found out that she did, an older man who was a cousin of a neighbor.

During the summer of 1984, Let committed an act of "losing face" that brought shame to our family. Out of nowhere on a Sunday afternoon, as Mom was on her way out of the house, she yelled at Lai and me, "*Soo nee heet hii jai koo kaat! (*You kids will give me a heart attack!)"

I had not heard my mother say that in a long time. Lai and I looked at each other, puzzled. We took off for Auntie's (Mom's youngest sister) who was very nosy. We knew she would know what had caused Mom to be so upset. Straightaway Auntie explained, "Your sister eloped."

For the rest of the day, our poor frantic mother went in and out of the apartment. By nighttime her eyes were glued to the door. Lai and I stayed up late with Mom and waited for Let to come home. Dad shut himself away in the bedroom.

"How could she do this to us?" Mom said many times, and looked over at Lai and me.

I couldn't help but curse Let, certain that our parents would now mistrust Lai and me. I could tell that Lai was thinking the same thing.

Let didn't come home that night. The next morning, the first words out of Dad's mouth were "She's no longer my daughter."

To him, Let's elopement was like a slap in the face, a disgrace to the family name.

For days after Let's elopement, our apartment was an unpleasant place to be. My father took his anger toward Let out on the rest of the family. I feared him so much that to avoid being a target, I hung out at other people's houses and went home only to sleep.

Almost a week later Mom received a call from an elderly man on behalf of Let and her boyfriend. "We will come to your house tomorrow to ask for your daughter's hand in marriage and for forgiveness," he told Mom. Mom couldn't say no and politely accepted the old man's offer.

"You can do as you please. I have nothing to say. She's not my daughter!" Dad, still angry at Let, said to Mom. She gave him a nasty look because of his unreasonableness and spent the whole day pestering him to forgive and not curse Let when he saw her. Dad kept his mouth shut.

The following month Let and her husband were married in our tiny apartment. Once again the marriage wasn't official in the eyes of California, but our community gave it their consent. It was a short ceremony with about thirty people. Afterward Let moved to San Luis Obispo, California, to live with her husband, Somchai.

As Lai and I feared, after Let eloped our father imposed stricter rules on us. Every time I asked permission to go out with friends, the standard response was "You can go, but remember, don't go and do what your sister did."

Poor Lai, since she was older, the scrutiny was more of a burden to her than to me. To escape the difficulties and the rules of our father's house, Lai also married young, at just age nineteen. After that she dropped out of junior college and soon had her first daughter, Christine. Two years later Donald was born, but at the age of two, he passed away from heart complications. A year and a half later, Matthew was born. Things weren't always rosy for Lai, but she and her husband overcame many hurdles to remain together as a family.

Now that we are adults, Lai and I are allies rather than foes. I connect with her more than anyone else in the family. She makes my life complete.

As for Let, despite the circumstances of her marriage, she and her husband turned out to be well matched. They have been married more than twenty years and have two kids, Annie and Andy. Much to my surprise, their marriage appears to be the best of the bunch.

* * *

As a teenager I wasn't the daughter that Dad and Mom wanted me to be. Our views of the world were like oil and water. They were rooted in their ways, and neither of us was willing to budge in our opinions, so we often clashed. I went along with many things that my parents instilled in me, and now that I'm an adult, I appreciate much of it. However, I can't forget how time and time again I was told that as a lady I couldn't do this or the other, such as with my involvement in sports; that was not the sort of thing that virtuous daughters did. My parents often did everything in their power to dissuade me from a lot of things I wanted to do, including going to college in Hawaii.

When I mentioned to Dad that I was considering that idea, he replied, "If you go, you will no longer be my daughter." He went on, "Why can't you be like the other kids? Why do you have to be different?

Why don't my kids listen to me?" The more he ranted, the more upset he got. "A proper young lady doesn't go off on her own!" He was almost yelling at that point.

"Why did I even bring this up?" I yelled back at him and stormed out of the house.

"He didn't mean it," Mom told me when I later shared with her my frustrations with Dad and how he'd threaten to disown me. I often had to remind myself that he was brought up in a different time and place, and his old age made him resistant to change. So when my father calmly suggested that I look for a job instead of attending college, I didn't get angry or frustrated with him. I understood his concerns about money since it was a constant struggle in our family.

To understand my father's rationale about most things, I had to read between the lines and remember the love he carried for us. Ever since I was a child, Dad's actions had always been the same. At every meal he always saved the best piece of meat for his children, so we could have the best of what was on the table. And there are the hundreds of times he tried to heal us when we were ill with chants, betel nuts, and the saliva. As a child I honestly believed his cures worked, although as an adult I can see that his healing powers were not what I once thought they were. Still, these gestures touched me deeply. I call it *love healing*.

Prospects

From third grade on to my high school graduation, I rarely thought about Cambodia, the camps, and other childhood memories. I put all of my energy into becoming a normal kid. Cambodia was in the past. The camps were in the past. Even Ai Sang Thout was in the past. Thoughts of him would appear and quickly disappear. If asked about him, I would briefly explain and change the subject. His death made me feel once again the remnants of Khmer Rouge brutality and our struggles in Cambodia.

In the fall of 1988, I started college as a sociology major at California State University of Hayward. To avoid more conflict with Dad, I opted for a local school rather than pursue Hawaii. It took me five years to get my degree and during that time I moved a few times—first to the campus, then to living at Lai's, and then back to living with Mom and Dad who by that time had moved in with Let.

While living on campus, I volunteered as a tutor and counselor to Asian youth in my spare time. While a college sophomore, I was hurting for money and had to swap volunteering for a paying job in the mail-order department of a major department store. While working there I discovered, much to my distress, that a T-shirt by a well-known designer could cost as much as a hundred dollars, an amount of money that could

127

feed my whole village back in Cambodia. My job was to carefully pack each item and make it as presentable as possible using tissue paper and fancy bows, items I considered to be an utter waste in terms of time and money. Even now I would find it appalling.

A year later the department store went out of business, and I was jobless and again struggling to get by on the financial aid I got for school. It covered the tuition but barely covered the gas to take me from place to place. To get by I depended on help from family and rarely bought anything that wasn't practical. From an early age and through necessity, I had learned to be very frugal and never spend beyond my means. I knew that we were all poor, so I never took advantage of my parents or Lai, the people I felt comfortable asking for money. Indirectly, Let also helped me out by having Mom and Dad live with her.

Still, we all had to find ways to get by. By then my parents were of an age that qualified them for Social Security. Let and her husband moved back to Oakland so Mom and Dad could look after their children and set aside some money. Lai received welfare support for herself and the kids, including subsidized housing in one of the worst neighborhoods in East Oakland, just a few blocks from the Oakland Coliseum. Crime and drugs dominated the neighborhood, especially inside the gated residential compound where she lived with about thirty other families. I lived with her in this two-bedroom apartment for my sophomore and junior years of college. It was an education in and of itself, although I must admit that I walked through the complex only once.

Lai laid down the security rules the day I moved in. "Make sure you securely lock the door behind you every time you come home," she warned. "I also want the windows completely closed and latched, and the curtains drawn shut."

Having lived in a crime-riddled environment for as long as I could remember, I knew to be vigilant, although my parents never failed to reiterate, "Make sure your car doors are locked and the car windows are closed when you drive through Lai's housing complex."

Being in Lai's apartment complex reminded me of the camp in Thailand, where after a while we were in constant fear. Somehow it seemed that no matter what country we were in or continent we were on, my family lived in dangerous circumstances.

A few years later my parents moved from the West Oakland apartment they had been in since coming to California. They and Let's family rented a cheap three-bedroom house near Lai's complex. It had been decided that my grandmother and I would move in with them as well. I wasn't happy about moving from one bad area to another, but I couldn't complain because I knew they couldn't afford anything better. So that year Grandma became my roommate, and she stayed my roommate even after we moved again when Let purchased a house in East Oakland in 1995. This time the neighborhood appeared decent.

A week after the move, someone knocked on our door. As always, Mom asked me to answer it because of her limited English.

I cracked the front door open, and said, "Yes?"

From the other side of the black security gate, a strange man made a strange request. "Ma'am, give me fifteen dollars please."

I was dumbfounded but remained collected as I asked him why.

"Ma'am, if you give me fifteen dollars, I will protect your family," he said. "I know your family just moved into this house, and you need someone to look after your whole family, otherwise you never know what some of the guys around here might do."

For a second I didn't know what to do or how to respond. My first instinct was to give him the money, so he wouldn't bother us.

"I only ask for fifteen dollars per month," he said, interrupting my thoughts.

This made me furious, but I didn't show it. I thought he might be insane, and I didn't want to get a crazy man upset.

"I can't give you the money," I calmly explained. "We're poor like you. We can't afford to give you what you've asked for. If we had money, we wouldn't be in this neighborhood."

"C'mon ma'am," he begged.

"No, and please leave. If you don't leave, I will call the police." With that I closed the door but stood on my tiptoes and squinted through the peephole, clutching the cordless phone. Luckily, the man left.

"What did he want?" Mom asked from another room.

"Just a crazy man begging for money," I told her. There was nothing to be gained by giving her the real story—that some thug tried to make us pay him to be our security guard. That would just keep her up all night. I changed the subject, but I noted the worried look on her face.

This new neighborhood was better than the previous one, but that wasn't saying much. Still, our family made this their permanent home. My father busied himself with turning most of the backyard into a tropical garden, growing herbs, chili peppers, limes, persimmons, bananas, and apples.

"Dad's going crazy in the yard," Let complained. "It's a mess!"

My father tends his garden every day, keeping the family supplied with herbs.

My Grandmother

I shared a room with my grandmother for about three years, up until I joined the Peace Corps and went off on my own. She was in her eighties; I was in my twenties. I didn't mind having my grandmother as my roommate as she and I had always gotten along.

Mao Tao V (Grandma V) was born and raised in Ban Doug Alaan, our village in Cambodia. Her given name was V Chalermchai. She married twice. The first marriage didn't last long after their only child was born, my Auntie Hien, the aunt who stayed behind in Cambodia to look after her stepfather. My grandmother met her second husband, my grandfather, after the first marriage ended. Until he met Grandma, my grandfather had been a monk. She was at least fifteen years his junior when she married him.

Like the other villagers of her generation in Cambodia, my grandmother believed that monks taught many of the great lessons in life. Therefore, it was important to her that her grandsons marked their rite of passage into manhood by becoming novices. When Dad permitted Ai Sang Thout to go through such a respected ritual, she was overjoyed. With so much work to do on the farm, she didn't think Dad would allow it.

"In my days," she once explained to me with great seriousness, "a man wasn't a man without completing his novice training. You are not to repeat that to your father. He missed that opportunity since his family needed him on the farm."

Like Ai Sang Thout before me, after an argument with Dad, I often sought comfort from Grandma. Her words made everything calmer. She would offer me the same advice about my father that she once gave to Ai Sang Thout: "He's a man without Buddhist training, so don't blame him, *lug*-daughter."

My grandmother was always there for her family—children and grandchildren alike. Even as she became toothless and wrinkled in her old age, to me, her sunken cheeks were adorable. She kept her beautiful gray hair cut short in a manly fashion. Dad trimmed her hair each month in our backyard. What I remember most about her appearance, though, were her elongated ears, like those I've seen on statues of Buddha. Years later, after grandma passed away, I read a description about Buddha, and it said the elongated ears represented wisdom. This made me think of Grandma, and it made me smile.

* * *

From decades of chewing betel nut, my grandmother's mouth was the color of dark burgundy. She and the other Nyaw women her age would go insane if they had to go a day without it. Grandma chewed betel nuts at least four times per day, if not more. It was the one pleasure in life that couldn't be taken away from her.

I can still conjure the vision of her and the other ladies in a pagoda during a *bun*, sitting on the floor in a circle, worshipping the betel nut chew set in the center. A *bun* is a festival celebrating the New Year, marriages, births, deaths, and so forth. Sometimes a *bun* is held at someone's house and sometimes at a Buddhist pagoda, and it usually lasts two days or more. No matter where it takes place, monks must be present to bless the event, and the entire Nyaw community would be invited.

In the States our neighbors were never happy when a *bun* was on. They complained about the heavy traffic and the noise, which could be ten times worse than a frat party. The *bun* literally took up a whole block, with cars parked every which way and as if there was no rule of law. Women and men drank alcohol openly, and kids ran amok. The constant flow of many people coming and going; the blaring music; people yapping in Cambodian, Lao, Nyaw, and English; and the odors of spices pouring from kitchens were unbearable for our neighbors. After several warnings from the local police, we learned to tone down the noise and forewarned our neighbors when another *bun* was on the way. Growing up I almost never missed a *bun* because it was the only time my parents didn't fuss about me staying up late. My friends and I took full advantage of the opportunities the occasion gave us to do the things that teenagers like to do.

For the elders, like Grandma, the "betel nut social circle" lasted throughout the *bun*. Every now and then someone would spit red juice into a can. Back in the village, that red juice would be spat on the temple ground or the floor of someone's house and nobody minded. In the States, however, each member of the social circle carried around her own can for spitting out the thick red betel juice. At times (and this happened very often) their aim was a bit careless and the juice would stain the carpet, the wall, or the hardwood floor. It was hard to clean.

Besides the betel nuts, Grandma enjoyed the occasional cigarette. Before smoking it she rubbed the cigarette with Tiger Balm so it would give off the aroma of mint as she puffed. Grandma also never turned down the offer of a shot of whiskey. In fact, she did a lot of leisure drinking when she lived with another auntie in San Diego, California, during her first few years in the States.

"Let her drink, because that's what keeps her going," my cousins often said, followed by a room full of laughter.

"Here, Grandma, I poured some whiskey for you," someone would say.

"*Er* (Yes)!" She would accept, grinning from ear to ear.

133

My parents were not too keen about her drinking habit, so when Grandma lived with us, her access to whiskey was drastically reduced. However, when there was a bottle of the stuff in the house, my grandmother had her shot every evening after dinner.

* * *

America was far removed from my grandmother even though she lived in it. She didn't know a word of English, and she never expressed a desire to venture outside our community. Having grown up in a place where she consulted the village shaman or a monk for remedies to treat her illness, receiving help from a doctor was a foreign concept to her—as were dentures, something we suggested she get. From many years of not having teeth, Grandma had mastered the art of gumming her food, but since we were in America now, we thought dentures would help her eat.

However, my grandmother disagreed. "I don't want fake teeth. Why would you people want me to have such thing?" she said utterly appalled.

"In America it's what people do. It will help you chew those tough meats."

"I don't want them!" she declared, and that was that.

Her sight, however, was a different matter. She had developed cataracts in both eyes. Even though she resisted, we insisted she see a doctor.

"I don't want the surgery. Just take me to the temple and have the monk bless me with holy water," she protested.

"Grandma, the doctor told me that your condition is good, and that he can help you see again," I said. She became quiet, her eyes sad and pleading.

"It'll be all right," I consoled, keeping my eyes averted.

A week after the consultation, I took her in for the first surgery to correct one of her eyes.

"You must stay very still and don't move," I said, repeating the doctor's instruction as the assistant strapped Grandma's head in place. After the anesthesia kicked in, I reluctantly left her in the surgery room.

"Does it hurt?" I asked her when she came to.

"*Bhor* (No)," she said as her hands grasped mine for support.

"The doctor said tomorrow we can take the patch off, and you should be able to see a bit," I said to reassure her.

"*Er, lug.* (Yes, daughter.)" I held her hand extra tight, as if to apologize for putting her through this ordeal. To clear my guilty conscience, I needed her to be well and for the surgery to be a success.

The next day my concerns were lifted. To anyone who came to see her, she said with a smile, "Is that you?"

That was when we learned that she had been almost completely blind. We had no idea that her sight had become that bad. The following week Grandma didn't resist going back for the second surgery on the other eye.

* * *

When I was about three years old, I scared Grandma nearly out of her wits. I had just woken up from an afternoon nap, and was still groggy and slow to move. As I sat with Mom eating a light snack, I heard Lai and cousin Chai giggling beside our house. To my delight, they were playing with unusual-looking dolls made from banana tree trunks. Usually we made dolls from mud, so I had never seen anything like them. I preferred the mud, but Lai and Chai so enjoyed their new dolls that I wanted to join in.

Smiling as I approached them, I cleared my throat and asked them with the utmost respect, "May I play?"

"No!" Lai snapped. Chai said nothing, just smiled at Lai. I begged and pleaded. I even went down on my knees and bowed with my palms clasped together, but they turned their backs to me, irritated and scornful.

"Go away!" Lai repeated several times.

I tried a different approach next, one a kid my age would use on a sibling who refused to cooperate: I sobbed. Softly at first, but when that didn't work, I cried louder and louder until, as expected, Mom yelled from the house.

"Lai, be nice to your sister!" I got an evil glare from Lai and Chai.

"If you shut up right now, we might let you play with us, but before you can, you must make a doll of your own because we are not sharing ours," Lai said.

Happy just to be given a chance to play, I rushed into the kitchen to fetch a butcher knife. It occurred to me even at that age that maybe I shouldn't use a knife, but the urge to play with Lai and Chai was so great that the cautious thought quickly vanished.

Lai, with an air of superiority, pointed to a pile of banana trunks and said, "There, make your own doll," and turned her back on me to carry on her play with Chai.

Not having a clue as to how to chop up the banana trunks, I struggled. The first and second attempts barely made a dent. On the third try, I used all my strength. *Thump!* Then I felt a tingling sensation. For a second I didn't get why half of the nail on my left thumb was missing. When I saw blood splatter everywhere, I turned white and the pain hit me. I shrieked so loud that I think I startled the whole village.

Mom rushed from the house and Grandma came running, hollering, "What! What happened to my daughter?"

As Grandma raced over, she became tangled in her sarong and it came apart. Her hair was in disarray, and the burgundy betel juice dripped down from both sides of her mouth. She looked like a mad woman.

Mom scooped me up and took me to the kitchen to rinse my finger in water. Grandma emptied the betel nut from her mouth and began to chew briskly a handful of tobacco. A minute later she took the tobacco from her mouth and placed it on my wound and bound it in place with a piece of cloth. The tobacco juice made my whole body sting, and I believe my cries once again startled the village. About thirty minutes later and still choking on tears, I sputtered to Mom and Grandma about what happened. Grandma scolded Lai and Chai and chased them away.

"*Sue Nee!* (You kids!)" Mom exclaimed as Grandma shook her head in disappointment.

When I calmed down, I asked them if my thumb would grow back, just like it was before.

"Yes, *lug* (daughter)," Grandma said, and Mom nodded in agreement.

That little white lie lifted my spirits. In the months that followed, I waited for my thumb to return to normal, but it never did. I was left with half a nail on my left thumb. As a child I was ashamed of it. Just looking at it scared me. Now, though, my spirits lift from this imperfection, because it brings with it this memory of my grandmother.

* * *

Despite the many humorous and tender memories that I have of my grandmother, I'm also aware of her hardships and sacrifices. At the time we needed to escape Cambodia, Grandma was physically strong and could walk great distances. My grandfather, though, was already old and unable to venture outside the village. My relatives discussed the pros and cons of her leaving Cambodia without him. In the end it was decided that she would escape with us, but Grandpa would remain.

Grandma's eldest daughter, Auntie Hien, stayed behind to care for Grandpa. Technically, Grandpa was her stepfather, but that distinction didn't matter. Grandpa died a year after we escaped. Auntie Hien and her husband died about two years later. We were told that Auntie Hien's husband was taken away and never heard from again. She later learned that he had been killed. Soon after that Auntie Hien became sick and died.

The morning we fled to Thailand in 1975 was the last time my grandparents saw each other. I have often wondered what their last words to each other were, but Grandma never talked about it. She would get very short with me when I ventured to ask if it was hard for her to leave him and the village. All she would say is that he was very old and couldn't walk for long.

"But how do you feel about this?" I probed further. "Do you miss Grandpa or the village?"

My grandmother's expression as I kept at this line of questioning was difficult to decipher.

After a long pause, she said, "The families said I should escape with them, so I did."

I didn't press any further. I suspect Grandma didn't regret leaving Cambodia despite knowing that those who were left behind survived only a few years, including Grandpa, Baa Hien, and Baa Hien's husband. I imagine that she counted not her losses but her blessings at getting to spend many years with our families and cousins in the States.

The War Talk

When the Khmer Rouge took control of Cambodia in April 1975, I was about seven years old. Although I lived through the changeover, I didn't fully understand the scope and the consequences of the war until I was about twenty-one. Once the impact of the Khmer Rouge became clearer to me, I had so many questions about this terrible event in our lives that I wanted to discuss with my parents. The problem was that after years of avoiding this part of our past, I didn't know how to approach the topic with them.

As a teenager I didn't want to be associated with the war, let alone talk about it. I just wanted to be a typical teenager who didn't carry this war as more baggage. So I took the easy way out and never brought it up with my parents. Then again, they didn't initiate a conversation about it with me either.

Once I was an adult and finally had the courage to ask my parents about the war, getting information from them was like extracting a tooth. My questions always seemed to take my mother by surprise. She would give me a strange look, the same kind of look she would give to doctors when they asked what ailed her, a look that said, "Don't ask anymore because I am in pain here."

My father, on the other hand, was usually slow to respond, but once he found a topic he was passionate about, he would ramble on and on. I've heard his account of the escape many times, and no matter how much I try to get him to talk about some other aspect of the war, he inevitably sticks with the same version of the same story. I then just let him talk until he runs out of steam.

My dad could handle talking about the war, but getting him or my mother to talk about their feelings was another story. Like most Asian families, we don't discuss our *feelings*. Once I asked them how they felt when they had to leave the only home they had ever known.

"Here she goes again," Mom said, looking around for a door or some other means she could use to escape the subject. Then she heard a sound that gave her what she wanted. "Your dad can answer better than I can," she told me. "I heard a noise. I have to go see where it's coming from," and just like that she disappeared.

I looked over at Dad who called after her, "*Oy*, where are you going?" She was nowhere in sight. By then Let and her husband had just arrived, and he quickly rushed to open the door to welcome them and the distraction they provided.

PART IV
NEPAL

The Peace Corps

After I graduated from college in 1995 with a BA in sociology, I wanted to become a Peace Corps volunteer. For me, the Peace Corps was the obvious choice. I was itching for something new and had a burning desire to experience life outside my normal surroundings. Although the thought of living in another country scared me, the work itself called to me so strongly that no fear could deter me.

My interest in the Peace Corps began back when we lived in the refugee camp in Thailand. I admired the way the aid workers gave up a comfortable life to help others. I liked the way they embraced another culture, and tried to learn our language even though we laughed at their mistakes. I wanted to be courageous like them, so I made a personal commitment to offer my service one day, when and if I was able. That day came in February 1996.

Many times I was asked why I would put my life on hold to return to a poor country like the one I escaped. As far as I was concerned, that was exactly a reason to return. Besides, I wanted to experience from an adult perspective what it was like to live in a poor country, I wanted to immerse myself in new things, and I saw the volunteer work as an opportunity to bridge the gaps between cultures. Working for the Peace Corps didn't seem like sacrifice to me. Rather, it was a guarantee to enrich my life. Unexpectedly I later discovered that volunteering helped me heal old wounds and gave me some clarity about myself.

Approximately five months after I submitted my Peace Corps application and was accepted, a letter detailing my first assignment arrived. With shaking hands I ripped opened the envelope and skipped over the congratulations to the word, *Nepal*, written in bold.

"Nepal!" I screamed. Where in the world is that?

When I consulted the world map, Nepal seemed as faraway as it could get from California. Within ten minutes family and friends heard the news. My parents were not thrilled by my plans, but that was no surprise.

"Nepal?" Dad asked. I pointed it out on the map.

"Oh, India. Make sure you go and bathe in the Ganges River. You will receive many blessings," he said, nodding his head.

"The Ganges River is the most polluted river in the world. I can't do that, and plus that's located in India. I will be in Nepal, not India. It's next to it, see?" I clarified.

"Yes, we see," both Dad and Mom said. Years later I overheard both of them tell their friends I used to work in India.

Unlike when I was in high school, my parents didn't try to nag me into doing something else. In fact, they said very little about me leaving for Nepal. For fear of getting more lectures from them about what kind of daughter I should be, I avoided them. I felt terrible anyway because I knew that they didn't want me to leave.

The winter of 1996 was when I left for Nepal, and it was the first time I'd traveled outside the United States since arriving as a refugee in the summer of 1980. Lai and her family drove my parents and some relatives to see me off at the airport. I avoided making eye contact with Mom. The few times I did, I noticed the apparent worry lines on her face. I scanned the faces before me, but my focus was really on my dad's to detect any signs of his disappointment. Looking back, I think Dad and I were just too shy to say what we really wanted to say, so we chatted with other people rather than with each other. Avoidance was always a quality of my relationship with my father.

One of the Peace Corps staff nudged me, the signal that it was time for me to board the plane. I said my last good-byes.

Dad said,"*Lovang derr* (Be careful)," and forced himself to smile, my first and only hint that my father actually approved of my decision to embark on this journey. Mom and I looked in each other's eyes, and that was our good-bye.

About thirty-six Peace Corps volunteers traveled with me that day. Nervous and excited, we chattered to each other so persistently that we irritated the other passengers. The flight attendants pleaded with us to be courteous during that long flight. After the plane landed in Tokyo, we transferred to Thai Airways. It was during this four-hour flight from Tokyo to Bangkok that I had my first glimpse of what it was like to be in Asia again. Right away, many things seemed familiar. Information given during the flight was spoken in Thai rather than English. It exhilarated me to be able to translate Thai to English and understand the gist of what was being said. It felt sort of like I was privy to a secret.

The five monks sitting a few rows up from me were what really made the return to Asia hit home. Their orange robes and the way they sat in the nirvana pose made me think of Dad and Mom and all the times our family consulted them for guidance. Right then and there I had a flashback to the time the monk in Thailand predicted Ai Sang Thout's destiny. ("The stick has a good balance. It hasn't fallen.") I remembered the hope that sprang from his forecast, and also the sorrow of hopes shattered by the death ceremony. My mind revisited the death ceremony too. The chanting of the mantra and the powerful smell of incense played out in my head like it was yesterday. Something stirred inside me, so much so that I fought back tears.

For the very first time, I itched to talk about the parts of the past I had so long avoided, but not just with anyone, with someone who had links in common with mine. But there was no such person on the plane, and I felt so far removed from my fellow volunteers. I resorted to reflecting about things alone but in peace. This time, instead of feeling hatred and rage toward the Khmer Rouge and nursing resentment toward people who had more than me, I found myself acknowledging how fortunate I was.

As the plane descended toward the runway in Bangkok, I fidgeted in my seat. I was about to arrive in a country linked to my roots. I considered Cambodia, Laos, and Thailand to be my countries of origin, and immediately I felt a connection and kinship with them that was difficult to put into words. As I stepped out of Customs at Don Mueang Airport, I wanted to kiss the ground. I wanted to give hugs and shake everyone's hand even though custom frowned upon touching others in such a way. I refrained. Instead, in my mind I screamed, *I am back!*

I couldn't get enough of the faces in the large crowd waiting to receive their family and friends, these faces were the reflection of mine: jet-black hair, flat nose, round eyes, and petite ladies who were my height. Each of them physically reminded me of myself, or someone from the Asian community back at home in Oakland. It took all of my will power to hold back from approaching them and saying, "Hello, Uncle, Auntie, Grandma, or Grandpa." The different Thai dialects I overhead around me were music to my ears. I felt in sync with everything around me, like a piece of a puzzle that suddenly fits. For the first time in sixteen years I didn't stand out in a crowd. Rather, I looked like the norm.

That night my Peace Crops group stayed at a hotel connected to the airport. At dinnertime a few of us strolled to a restaurant near the hotel. My mouth watered from the aroma of the spices sold in the food stalls we passed. I heard kids shouting and laughing and playing, while grown-ups hollered threats for them to calm down. I understood it all, and I laughed out loud as I remembered receiving similar scolds as a child.

At the restaurant, knowing that it would be my last Thai supper for a very long time, I ate like it was my last meal. When the live band sang songs that I knew, I pinched myself to make sure I wasn't dreaming. I stood back and watched my fellow volunteers dance the night away with the locals. Hours later, when I was back at the hotel, I didn't want to close my eyes or go to sleep. I just wanted to savor these moments.

* * *

My first glimpse of the snow-covered Himalayas from the plane window left me awestruck. They were almost frighteningly beautiful. As the plane approached the airport in Kathmandu, the colors changed from white to a glorious mustard. Jodi, another Peace Corps volunteer, grabbed my hand and held it until the plane came to a halt. Although it was winter, the heat and humidity took me by surprise as I stepped off the plane. The thick air, the strange musty smell, and the small dusty airport made me feel off balance.

"Namaste(greetings),"The Peace Corps staff welcomed us after we had collected our bags and zigzagged our way through a mob of boys begging for pens.

We boarded a bus and were greeted by Kirk, another volunteer who had been in Nepal for a year. "This will be your nicest bus ride during your two years in Nepal," he said as he laughed. We all laughed with him nervously. Soon I would learn firsthand that Kirk was right. Most vehicles in Nepal were decrepit and should have been retired to a junkyard.

The streets of Kathmandu were chaotic. Shop after shop blasted Hindi music at top volume. Cars and buses constantly honked at people and animals in their way. Everything looked like it was in need of repair. The brick homes had chipped paint or missing parts. Huts leaned to their side and seemed on the verge of collapse. Stray dogs wandered everywhere in search of food with their heads down, as if afraid to look up. The cows, although held sacred, were skin and bones.

As strange as the scene was to me, I had a sense that I could relate to the people. In the refugee camps, I had been a kid like the ones I saw from the bus, dressed in rags with a dirty face and using my sleeves to wipe teary eyes or a snotty nose. While some of the other volunteers chattered loudly, I mulled over the realization that the bus driver and I were probably the only ones on the bus who had been as poor as the people we drove past.

The bus dropped us off at the Imperial Guest House located in the heart of Kathmandu called *Thamel*. I was glad to be there but dreaded the jet lag that was sure to come.

I was lost in my own thoughts when I heard a voice from behind me ask, "Would you like to be my roommate?" I turned around to see a fellow volunteer, Heather Atkinson. A tall, thin redhead, Heather towered over me.

"Yes!" I said without hesitation.

I met Heather on the evening before the flight to Nepal, during the Peace Corps meet-and-greet at a hotel in San Francisco. She was from Schenectady, New York, but had been living in Southern California prior to joining the Peace Corps.

After we unpacked our things, Heather and I joined the others for a quiet dinner after getting some guidance on where to go from an experienced volunteer. At dinner, though, jet lag, nerves, and excitement stole my appetite. I went to bed early, but the six o'clock wake-up call the next morning was still a nuisance. I was always one to keep hitting the snooze button, and if an alarm clock could talk, it would be exasperated from telling me repeatedly to wake my ass up.

Unlike me, Heather was an early riser, something I thought my mother would have loved about her. For my mother, it was important to wake up early. When I was growing up, she always said, "Wake up or all the ripe fruits will be gone." Lying in bed that first morning in Kathmandu, I imagined that Heather picked all the ripe mangoes from the lower branches, and I was left with the green sour mangoes at the top.

As I was still trying to avoid getting out of bed, I heard a loud pop. Then the lights blacked out, and I heard a shout from the bathroom. Groggy, I jumped from the bed, opened the curtain to get more light in the room, and rushed to the bathroom. When Heather opened the bathroom door, smoke poured out. I fanned it away and saw Heather's wet hair was tangled across her entire face, like a witch's experiment gone wrong.

"What happened? Are you all right?" I asked.

"Look, my blow-dryer," she said. Her hair dryer still smoked, and the room smelled of burnt electricity.

"I got the transformer, but why did the circuit still blow out?" she asked.

I couldn't help but chuckle as I mumbled that I didn't know.

She was fine, and I took over the bathroom while she stepped to the side. When I came out of the bathroom, Heather was drying her hair in a way unique to me. She stood with her legs akimbo, leaned over, and tossed her head back and forth, sending drops of water all over the room. She had long, thick hair that took forever to dry. After a bit she became dizzy and had to stop. Later that day someone commented about a blackout earlier that morning. Heather and I looked at each other, and we had a good laugh.

For the remaining two years in Nepal, Heather and I always shared hotel rooms whenever we were in the same town for a conference or a meeting. She was one of my closest Peace Corps friends. Years later after our Peace Crops service, Heather was diagnosed with cancer. She put up a good fight but lost the battle and passed away in the summer of 2008. She was about my age. Heather will forever be in my thoughts, and I cherish my memories of her.

Peace Corps/N-181-C, Nepal, 1996-1998

Prafulla and me in Pokhara,
Nepal, 1996.

Kalpana and me in Rajbiraj,
Nepal, 1997.

Rajbiraj

When people think of Nepal, they tend to think of the Himalayas. My Peace Corps assignment in the southeastern part of the country showed me how diverse the country could be. For two years I called Rajbiraj home. Rajbiraj is a mid-size town, in the flatlands of Terai, was just a stone's throw from the Indian border, comprised mostly of an ethnic group known as the Maithili.

One of my initial reservations about becoming a Peace Corps volunteer was that my host country wouldn't accept me because of how I looked. I was Asian and didn't match the picture of a typical American in the eyes of unworldly people. I wasn't light skinned, blue-eyed, and blonde. So when I first arrived in Rajbiraj, I was nervous that my appearance would be a hindrance. I soon learned that those notions had no merit. The people were indeed curious about my background, but they had no reservations about accepting me into their town.

For certain, my experiences would have turned out differently if not for my Nepalese counterpart, Prafulla Shrestha. All Peace Corps volunteers worked alongside a local person during their assignments.

"Welcome to Rajbiraj, Mai-ji!" Prafulla greeted me in perfect English the first time we met. In Nepal, a suffix "ji" is added after the name when addressing someone formally.

"*Dhanyabad* (Thank you)," I said, using the only Nepali word I was comfortable saying.

Prafulla and I worked at the municipality office doing youth development work. With support from the municipality's leading official and the Peace Corps, our task was to provide job training to youth at risk in Rajbiraj. Most of the time our efforts failed, I hate to admit, but now and again we did something right. It was these triumphant moments that kept us going.

"Mai-ji, you must have patience," he always reminded me when things were not going according to plan with our youth development project. "I've worked with Peace Corps volunteers for the past ten years, and I understand your frustration. Come, let's have some chai." Not a day went by that I didn't drink chai at least twice.

The groundwork for the youth training project in Rajbiraj would have been dead if not for Prafulla's patience and persistence. By the end of my service there, the program was up and running.

I felt at ease with Prafulla from the very first day I met him. Although he was in his late thirties, from a middle-class family, married, and the father of three, I easily confided in him about almost everything, from work to personal matters. Like any good friend, he listened and didn't belittle my sometimes naïve ways of thinking. We agreed on many levels about the things we discussed, a characteristic I found to be rare in a country that was very chauvinistic.

* * *

The two leading officials of Rajbiraj, the major and the vice major, were like night and day.

The major was a tall, dark-complexioned man in his mid-thirties who was always surrounded by his entourage. Whenever I passed him, we nodded to each other politely from afar and then went about our business. I think we had a mutual fear of each other. I was too timid to attempt to speak Nepali to a man in his position, and he was reluctant because of the language barrier. I believe I was among the first few foreigners he'd ever met.

The major was elected to his office for the first time not long after I arrived in Rajbiraj. Every person I met on the street of Rajbiraj gave me an earful about his background.

"He's humble," Prafulla said.

Unlike his predecessors, the major came from a very poor family in Rajbiraj and was not an outsider. He was elected on the assumption that he could relate to the poor people of the town.

The vice major, by contrast, came from a city called Biratnagar, which is the fourth largest city in Nepal, was of medium build, and had the look of a Don Juan about him. His mustache was always perfectly trimmed, and his shiny hair was parted to the side. Unlike the major who wore traditional clothing that resembled pajamas, the vice major dressed in western clothes, slacks always perfectly ironed and breezy shirts of assorted colors. Sometimes during the winter the vice major dressed in a suit, a rare thing for Rajbiraj.

The vice major spoke a little English, and he never hesitated to carry a conversation with me. He was interested in different parts of the world, and in our discussions we compared different cultures, our views on values, and so forth. On the wall of the vice major's office was a world map, and toward the end of my assignment, I noticed fingerprints and inks marks on Cambodia.

When introducing me to guests, the vice major always explained that I was an American Peace Corps volunteer working in his office. Inevitably his description received puzzled looks.

"How? She looks like one of us," someone always insisted, a question I heard all the time from the Nepalese.

When I traveled alone in Nepal, I went unnoticed, something I loved. Once I opened my mouth, heads turned and questions were fired at me. I had to do a lot of explaining about my background, how my life started in Cambodia, and how I wound up in America.

* * *

While I met many wonderful Nepali people who had an impact on me, only two were like a second family: Praffulla and Kalpana, the municipality secretary. At five feet tall Kalpana was a beautiful lady with perfect skin. Although a few years shy of my age, she was more like a protective older sister. In fact, she reminded me of Lai. Both were very frank and would do anything for me.

Kalpana knew everyone in Rajbiraj, so going to the market with Kalpana always took longer than usual. She stopped or waved at every stall and greeted people at every corner. I couldn't keep up with all the names and faces as we strolled the town hand in hand or arm in arm. The first time I felt Kalpana's hand I was struck by how different our lives were—her hand, toughened by hard work, felt like rough leather. She could move a hot iron pot with her bare hands.

Kalpana always made sure I had someone to be with or somewhere to be during the holidays. I'm a person who likes her solitude, but I would get lonely during the holidays if I didn't visit other Peace Corps volunteers or have them over to my place. When I was on my own, I cleaned, read, and paced as I prayed for the holiday to be over. Sometimes I found that weekends could also be unbearable if I was on my own the whole time. I would anxiously want Monday to come, so I could go to the office where there were some people to talk to or have chai with. Although I wasn't a smoker then (and I'm still not one now), I always kept a pack of cigarettes on hand for those lonesome times in Nepal. I may have finished a few packs of cigarettes during my time there.

Thank goodness Kalpana was there. I often found myself in her one-room flat during Nepali holidays. She would never allow me to help her prepare the food, no matter how much I begged, but I always kept her company in the kitchen. We talked about whatever came to our minds, using both English and Nepali words to communicate amid the spicy aromas of her cooking.

It's tradition in Nepal that the wife serves her husband and guests and waits until they're done before she eats. The first time she invited me over, I told Kalpana that although I was her guest, I refused to be served first and that we would eat at the same time.

"Mai-ji," she said, "that's not tradition."

"I'll wait. We'll eat together because in America and Cambodia, everyone eats at the same time, guests or no guests," I said.

Kalpana's husband shook his head. "Let us all eat together—Nepali, American, and Cambodian traditions," her husband said. I couldn't have agreed more.

From that day forward, that was how we both broke and merged traditions whenever I was at Kalpana's, and each meal was just as tasty as the first one. After dinner, while Kalpana cleaned, I attempted to play with her timid one-year-old son while her husband dug out his English book to practice it with me.

Kalpana also she made sure that I was properly dressed to attend functions. I often overheard her ask the other ladies in our office for advice on the matter.

"*Didi*(sister), what do you think Mai should wear?"

"She can borrow my red, green, and oh, the bright stripe orange sari with black top and…," they went on and on in whispers. Their attention made me feel really good inside.

Putting on a Sari was difficult, and I always needed help. Of course, it was Kalpana I turned to. I would stand like a mannequin while Kalpana and another *didi* wrapped, turned, pulled, and tucked. In the end I was dressed in a colorful sari that could be spotted a mile away, along with fancy earrings, multicolored bracelets, and a ring to match. I looked like a cast member of a Bollywood movie.

As I walked through the town in my sari and jewelry, the heat and humidity made me feel faint, but like an obedient little sister wanting to please her older sister, I didn't complain. Nor would I say that my blood wasn't circulating because my shirt was too tight, or that never in my life had I worn such colorful clothes. In my head I heard my mother's voice say, "You mustn't complain when others are showing their kindness toward you." This lesson of my mother's paid off on many occasions in my life, but mostly during my years in Nepal.

Before I left Rajbiraj to return home to the States, Kalpana took me to her village. I'd met all of her family when they were in town, but I had not had the opportunity to visit her village in the most remote part of Rajbiraj. We went in late February, during the time the rice crop is at its young stage. After about an hour riding in the back of a pickup truck on a potholed dirt road, we walked hand in hand another mile through the rice paddies. Off in the distance, Kalpana's neighbor greeted her, and she waved back. When we finally arrived at her family's house, her mother squatted in front of some cow dung that she'd prepared for mending their mud hut. The cow dung was already well mixed with water to soften it.

After our cordial *Namaste*, she went back to tend to her work. Kalpana fetched me a stool and disappeared into the kitchen to make chai. I sat next to the somewhat smelly dung pile watching Kalpana's mother fill in every crack and every hole in the wall, carefully and expertly applying the dung with her hands. When the dung dried, the wall of the mud hut looked smooth. I had seen this done many times and knew that it was a weekly task for them, if not daily.

As Kalpana gave me a tour of the compound, we ate biscuits, drank chai, and she explained that all of her extended family lived here.

"Those two huts are for sleeping. That one is a barn for our animals. That hut is our kitchen," she said, pointing to each of the four mud huts that surrounded us.

We spent half the day with Kalpana's family. By then Kalpana's mom had moved from fixing the mud hut to tending her abundant garden. With palms together, I bid her *"Namaste* (good-bye)."

When I got home late that afternoon, I reflected about my time spent in Nepal. I was leaving in a few weeks, and the thought of that overwhelmed me. To calm my nerves, I sat quietly on my balcony smoking a cigarette, watching the geckos on my wall chase each other, thinking about all I had witnessed in Nepal in the past two years, its beauty, its sadness, and its hopefulness.

* * *

I think I was meant to be in Nepal and that I was there for all the right reasons. I instantly fell in love with the country and the people. Nepal is the country where Lord Buddha was born and where ancient temples are adorned with deities and goddesses. Shamans, hippies, and lost souls go there to seek enlightenment. I like the exotic sound of the capital, *Kath-man-du*, the way the syllables flow from my mouth. I even like the abbreviation—*K'du*. I dove into Kathmandu and came up feeling like Nepal had baptized me.

In so many ways and so often, Nepal reminded me about my past and the kind of life our family had led in the village in Cambodia. Whenever I saw Nepali children roaming the hills, I remembered how I too had once been so carefree. Before the war there were no limits to how far kids could venture within or outside the village. Barely clothed, we chased after animals, swam in a lake filled with leeches, climbed trees to pick wild fruit, or hunted for insects to eat. We had little super-vision or no supervision, just as I saw with Nepali children.

In Rajbiraj I lived in a third floor, three-bedroom apartment with a beautiful balcony that overlooked the whole neighborhood. I liked being on the balcony at nighttime the best, because I could gaze out into the dark night and listen to the night sounds. The twinkling stars provided some light and made me feel calm inside. In the huts around me, candles flickered; and during the winter the fireflies swarmed around the fruit trees, making them look magical, like decorated Christmas trees. There was no sound of traffic, no electricity humming in the background, and no phone calls. Such nights were therapeutic, allowing me to reflect on the past as well as the present.

Living in America had made me forget a lot about the very basic things humans do to survive, but living in Nepal brought me back, you could say, to the beginning of things. From my third-floor *dhera* (home), I could hear my neighbors go about their lives: the smell of spices waft-ing up from their tiny kitchens, a newborn crying, or the sound of water splashing from people taking an evening shower or cleaning the dishes. Those things took me back in time. The sights and sounds of Nepal struck a familiar chord, reminding me greatly of my village in Cambodia and how connected I was to everyone around me. I could clearly see Mom and I squatting next to the open fire, waiting patiently for the food to cook, and sometimes she would give me the best piece of meat to taste. I could recall the sounds of splashing water as my dad took his evening shower, or Let washed the dinner dishes.

I will always be grateful for my time in Nepal, because without it I wouldn't fully appreciate what I have, and I wouldn't know who I am. I've since visited other countries, most of them only once, but I know I will keep returning to Nepal, a place where all my experiences amount to good notes in my diary and in my memories.

First Trip Back

After I completed my service in the Peace Corps in April 1998, I met up with Dad, Uncle Oun (Dad's younger brother from Canada), Mom, and Lai in Bangkok. From there we crossed the border into Cambodia. It had been nearly twenty-three years since we left the country.

To my surprise, the sight of men in uniform hurled me back in time to when as a child I hid from the Khmer Rouge in my house. In my mind these soldiers looked the same as those of the Khmer Rouge who came through the villages. These were the faces that Dad said to stay away from and the faces who might have taken away Ai Sang Thout in handcuffs, his head hanging low. That was (and still is) how I envisioned Ai Sang Thout's surrender.

To make matters worse, Uncle Oun hired five soldiers to escort us from the border of Thailand to Siam Reap. Had the soldiers not traveled with us, I would have been able to reflect on what it meant to be back in Cambodia again. Instead I was on guard and anxious. The roads were in the same shape as the country: terrible. Every time the truck hit a pothole my insides churned, and having the soldiers there only made my worries worse. The few times I made eye contact with the soldiers, I instantly smiled and looked away. It was what I had been instructed to do as a seven-year-old child before we fled Cambodia, so that I wouldn't cause trouble or bring unwanted attention to the family. My father's words rang in my head: "This is a way to be safe."

"It is still not safe to travel here," Uncle Oun explained when I questioned with irritation why we needed the soldiers with us.

In Siem Reap early the following morning, Lai and I were anxious to see the famous Angkor Wat temple. We had never seen it before. I convinced Lai to ditch the soldiers and go off on our own, while my parents decided to stick with Uncle Oun and the armed escort. We hopped onto the back of our tour guide's motorbike, and we looked a lot like the locals zigzagging the streets and alleys of Siam Reap at a clip. I had a panic attack every time our bike dodged other bikes, cars, people, and animals, but once the crowd and traffic were behind us, I enjoyed the rush of being on a motorbike speeding down the road.

As we entered the temple grounds, a line of trees and statues greeted us from both sides. For the next four hours I marveled at everything. The stories carved on the walls—stories of pride, wars, and struggles—spoke to me.

In the main temple of Angkor Wat, I found myself surrounded by statues that stared back at me no matter where I stood and at every angle. Scanning the faces of each statue, I wondered what they were there to say and what purpose they served. Being in the temple was a mystifying experience, which I kind of liked. By contrast, the dancers carved on the walls behind the statues read like the cover of a book. They were the chosen few who had mastered the popular art of a Khmer classical dance called the Apsara and entertained royalty. For each figure, the symbols that showed their status was carefully carved in perfect duplication, yet upon a closer look, each one had its own characteristics—voluptuous, curvy bodies, perfect breasts, and the broad lips that Khmer women are known for having.

While I admired the statues, Lai made merit (gave alms) at every figure missing a head or a limb.

"I feel the need," she said when I became impatient with having to wait for her and gave her "the look."

"Mai, come sit next to me to give alms. At least do it a few times and pray for whatever you want," she suggested.

"With the way you're giving alms, you'll soon join the beggars," I joked with her. We had a good laugh, but minutes later she was back to giving alms. On her knees and with a stick of burning incense in her hands, Lai prayed like the world was coming to an end. She kneeled side by side with the locals, but unlike the locals, she slipped money into the donation box before we moved on to the next statue that had lost its face or arm or leg.

Later that evening we joined my parents at another temple ground in Siem Reap. As we rested in the shade and watched Cambodian kids try to sell trinkets to tourists, my father said, "Pol Pot is dead."

It took a few seconds for those words to sink in. It was hard to believe that a man responsible for the death of almost 2 million Cambodians had himself just died. Dad repeated his statement, and that was when I wanted to shout with joy at the top of my lungs, raise my arms into the air in celebration, and sing like I had the spirit in me, as my ESL teacher had once told me to do. I wanted to rally and celebrate his death, like the way some Americans rallied together at Ground Zero or at the White House after Osama Bin Laden was killed.

To my dismay no one else seemed excited by the news. Lai tugged my shirt and reminded me that the Khmer Rouge was still in control. "You mustn't express much while we're here!"

I was disappointed to hear that, and for the rest of the day, I thought of Ai Sang Thout. I told him the good news and wanted him to know that it was the beginning of justice. Lai and I chatted about the event, but most of the time my mind wandered and wondered if Pol Pot's death was satisfying enough.

We left Siem Reap early the following morning. This time there were only two soldiers, rather than five, to escort us back to Thailand, which was a major relief to me. We made one last stop at the Angkor Wat temple, and this time there wasn't a soul there besides us. Under the morning mist, the temple looked untouched and majestic.

I suggested we take photos of my parents with the temple in the background, but Mom protested.

"I don't want to stop. Let's get out of here," she said in a stern voice.

That was when I realized that my mother didn't feel at all sentimental about Cambodia and wanted no part of it. I felt a twinge of guilt, because I was the one who had insisted that we visit Angkor Wat.

It took us about three hours to get from Siem Reap to Battambang. In Battambang we stayed at a hotel that looked more like a prison. The whole place was barricaded with barbed wire, and all of the rooms had security gates for the windows and doors.

"Make sure to be indoors before the sun goes down, and completely shut the doors and windows," Uncle Oun said as he left to spend the night at the home of the soldiers. Poor Mom, these instructions did not give her any peace of mind. She tossed and turned all night long.

When we again left early the following day, I thought we were headed straight for the border, but then the truck turned left onto a red dirt road leading to the village of my birth, Ban Doug Alaan. It was a pleasant surprise. No one in the village expected a visit from us, and once we arrived Mom and Dad recognized familiar faces right away. People slowly emerged from their huts and shacks, and the next thing I knew we were surrounded by relatives. In the few hours that we were there, I met cousins I never knew I had. They welcomed us and paraded us to different homes so my parents had a chance to speak to everyone briefly.

Our old house still stood smack dab in the heart of the village. I learned that it was among the few houses that made it through the time of the Khmer Rouge. It looked almost exactly like I remembered it, except that it seemed smaller and the kitchen connected to the house was missing.

"Can we ask the family who's living there if I can go inside the house?" I asked.

"No, we don't know them well, and it's best that we don't," a cousin said.

Instead Mom, Dad, Lai, and I, along with some of our cousins, stood on the other side of the dirt road staring across at the house my parents built with their own hands. Memories played out in my head of the pigs, the fruit trees, and the steps I used to sit on. My index finger touched my half thumb, and I saw the very spot at which part of my thumb was chopped off. The palm trees on the side next to an aunt's house were still standing. I didn't want to move on with the others. I wished there was a cafe next to where I was standing from which I could unobtrusively take pictures of the house or sketch it, or just sit there for however long and reminisce. However, when a man appeared in front of the house and stared at us suspiciously, Lai dragged me away. We quickly ran to catch up with the others.

It had been over twenty years since I left the village, and we only had three hours to spend in it, because we had to hurry and cross the border back to Thailand. That day in April was at the tail end of the Cambodian New Year celebration, and as we walked from the edge of Cambodia into Thailand, a few people splashed water on us to wish us Happy New Year. Exhausted from the trip, I didn't respond to the well wishes bestowed upon us. All I could think about was why the news of Pol Pot's death was not enough to satisfy me.

* * *

After the trip to Thailand and Cambodia, I returned to Oakland. I didn't slip seamlessly back into life in the States. The adjustment took some time. For months all I did was share pictures of and tell stories about Nepal. When I was sure my family and friends grew sick of this, I reached out to other Peace Corps volunteers who had returned to the US. That helped me ease back into society, but I soon found that life in the States was dull. I learned to accept that, yet I was always itching for an opportunity to go overseas again.

That opportunity almost came in the form of a position to teach English in Japan. I interviewed for the job, but in the meantime had met the man who would become my husband through work at the Immigration and Naturalization Service (INS) in San Francisco. Our relationship blossomed at lightning speed, and eight months later Peter and tied the knot in Bangkok. In that same year, with a goal to ultimately take a post overseas, Peter accepted a position in Washington, DC. After two years in DC, we had our daughter, Sophie. When Sophie was a little over a year, Peter accepted a position to work at the US Consulate office in Hong Kong as immigration attaché. Once again I could return to Asia. I quit my job and, for the next three years, became a stay-at-home mom in Hong Kong.

PART V
THE SEARCH FOR AI SANG THOUT

Possibilities

've been back to Cambodia many times since the visit with my parents in 1998, but for a long time I purposely avoid Phnom Penh. I didn't want to be in a place where everything was a reminder of the war, particularly the notorious S-21 prison where Cambodians were imprisoned, tortured, and killed by the Khmer Rouge. I knew that one day I would make that visit, but I put it off knowing that I would scrutinize photos of the prisoners on display, hoping and praying that I would recognize Ai Sang Thout among the fearful faces staring back at me. I had a habit of doing that whenever I came across something that reminded me of him.

I recall one such occasion while living in Hong Kong. Peter had just returned home from a business trip to Bangkok. As always, he went to one of his favorite places in Bangkok, the Asia Bookstore. Peter loved to read. Since marrying me we had accumulated all sorts of books about Asia. From this trip he brought back a book titled, *Saigon 1975: Three Days and Three Months* by Tiziano Terzani. The picture of a soldier on the cover made me take a double look. I searched the soldier's face for a while but then stopped. *Nah, it couldn't be*, I said to myself, as I placed the book back on the coffee table and went to check on Sophie in the bath.

But as I played with Sophie, still splashing about in the tub, my mind kept returning to the book. It took place in Vietnam but during the same period that the Khmer Rouge took over Cambodia. I went back into the living room to fetch the book and brought it back to the bathroom, so I could look at it again but still keep an eye on Sophie. While she played with her "pretend" boat made from peanut shells, I studied the picture on the cover. The soldier resembled Ai Sang Thout.

The soldier sat on some steps with a serious look on his face. He appeared to be the same age as Ai Sang Thout would have been at the time the photo was taken. What struck me the most about the soldier's face, besides his overall features, was his mouth. A few of the Bunla family members had thick upper heart shaped lips. The soldier on the cover of the book had that same feature.

Anxious and hungry for any answer as to the fate of my brother, I read the author's bio, praying for the impossible. Although the author had immense experience covering war stories all over the world, his bio made no mention of him in Cambodia. Still, my thoughts focused on the possibility that he might have been in Cambodia and that he could have taken some photos there. And maybe, just maybe, the face on the book cover was Ai Sang Thout.

Seeing Sophie was comfortable sinking her peanut shell boats in the tub, I went into the living room to compare the photo on the book cover to the only picture I had of Ai Sang Thout. *Yes,* I told myself, *this man in the cover picture could be Ai Sang Thout,* but I knew it was wishful thinking. When Peter came into the room and asked me what I had in my hands, I felt embarrassed.

"The book you brought from Bangkok," I answered.

"That's a very good book. And a remarkable author. You should read it when you have time," he said.

"Yeah," I said. I didn't tell Peter the reason behind my curiosity. I quickly put the book down and returned to Sophie in the tub.

Thinking I would come across information about Ai Sang Thout was a common occurrence for me, particularly while living in Hong Kong. It was there that I made my first attempt to find him. I met a couple, Kate and Rada, who ultimately became my link back to Cambodia and sparked my interest in searching for my brother. Rada was born and raised in Cambodia during the time of the Khmer Rouge.

During our many get-togethers with Kate and Rada at our apartment in Hong Kong, so far removed and different from Cambodia, our discussions were mainly about Cambodia. We talked about the genocides and human rights violations. We expressed our revulsion at the ongoing corruption but also our awe at the strength of spirit in the Cambodians who outlived the Khmer Rouge legacy. With the exception of Rada, the rest of us felt our strength in overcoming obstacles paled in comparison to that of the Cambodians who survived the Khmer Rouge.

Out of the goodness of their hearts, Kate and Rada assisted me with my first attempt to find information about Ai Sang Thout. They were going to Cambodia for a visit. I was very excited about the search but also reserved, wanting to protect myself from old wounds. I didn't want to stir something in me that had been calm and forgotten for decades.

In the days leading up to Kate and Rada's departure, I scribbled a short bio about Ai Sang Thout. Rada later translated the bio into Khmer so it could be advertised in the Cambodian newspaper. The printed translation appeared beautifully written. I found myself getting emotional as I stared at the writing that looked like Sanskrit and the black-and-white photo of Ai Sang Thout next to it. I allowed myself to cry that day, something that hadn't happened in a very long time.

A few days later, on a hazy afternoon in Hong Kong, my mobile rang just after Sophie and I had returned from our errands. I didn't recognize the number. I hesitated to answer it, but I clicked the answer button and reluctantly said hello.

"Hi, Mai!" I was relieved to hear Kate's voice on the other end. She sounded excited and right away told me that the Khmer Surlang Newspaper agreed to print the ad about Ai Sang Thout for one month. So many thoughts ran through my mind, I didn't know what to do except thank Kate profusely. After I hung up the phone, I shook with emotion. I desperately needed some time to myself. I plunked Sophie in front of the TV and disappeared into the bathroom, where I allowed myself to cry and ask, *Why haven't I done this sooner?*

After a good cry, I was composed once again, and I wanted to share my endeavor and hopes with the world. Or at least with Lai, but since it was 3:00 a.m. her time, I didn't. Later that night (Hong Kong time), I called my parents and told them about what I'd done. As usual it was hard to read Mom, but the fact that she probed for more information made me think that she was interested. Dad seemed a bit reserved, as if he knew nothing would come from the ad. He had the right to think so, but I allowed myself to still feel excited and hopeful. I phoned Lai later that same morning. As we spoke I knew we were on the same wavelength, and that both of us were afraid to express our fears. Instead we held our breath and chatted on.

The following day I begin to muse about how I would deal with the outcome of the ad. Say, if someone came forward and informed us of Ai Sang Thout's death, how would I feel then? Would I grieve all over again? If so, how would that be different from the first time?

And if Ai Sang Thout were alive, his life would be completely different from mine—what was that life like? Did he become a soldier? Did he live a life under constant scrutiny? If he was forced to join the revolution, what did he have to do to convince the regime to let him live? How far did he have to go to demonstrate to the Khmer Rouge regime he was more valuable alive than dead? Did he become the kind of Khmer Rouge responsible for taking many lives? Thinking about this made me ask myself a very disturbing question: is there some Khmer Rouge in all of us? To what extent will humans go when it's a matter of life and death?

Two weeks after the ad appeared in the newspaper, we received word that a man had contacted Rada's brother, Channa, claiming to be Ai Sang Thout. Channa sent me a message right away, but he sounded skeptical, because the man in question appeared to know very little when he was questioned over the phone. Kate and Rada had since returned to Hong Kong, so I asked Channa to meet with the man. Channa and I spoke and exchanged e-mails a few times to prep him about what questions to ask.

The day of the meeting between Channa and the man claiming to be my brother was the most anxious day of my life. With sweaty palms, jaw tight, and every muscle knotted with tension, I paced our apartment.

Kate and Rada came over to wait for the news with me, while Peter kept Sophie occupied. When Rada's phone finally rang, we all jumped. It was Channa. I could hear his voice but couldn't make out what he said.

"No, Mai. It's not your brother," Rada said to me with the phone still hanging onto his ear.

"Who is this man?" I asked.

"He said he is from Don Rung village where he'd been raised by his grandparents after he lost his family during the war," Rada said.

"Oh, OK" was the only thing that I could think to say at that moment. Apparently this man was also named Thout, and he had had four siblings. His parents and siblings were said to have died during the time of the Khmer Rouge, but he had held out hope that we were his family. When asked for their names, he said he couldn't remember them.

Clearly, the man who had come forward was not my Ai Sang Thout but a desperate man who had lost his family during the war. I was disappointed but held no ill will toward him, given the circumstances. It made me sad to think that he longed for a family, just as I was sure that Ai Sang Thout longed for us.

No one else came forward in response to the newspaper ad, even though it aired on Cambodian radio and was posted in the "Missing" section at the Cambodian Documentary Center.

Conclusion

I am who I am because of what I have experienced, witnessed, and lived through. The past affects my decisions daily. Numerous articles, memoirs, and stories have been collected about the Khmer Rouge. The impact they had on my life has been duplicated on countless other lives. Every Cambodian has his or her own Khmer Rouge story to tell, and even if our stories are similar, they deserve to be told by various people of various backgrounds. These tales of immeasurable pain, infinite suffering, and extraordinary endurance and tolerance need to be preserved so the world can bear witness to what happened in Cambodia. To this day, I don't have to look far to be reminded of the war. The Khmer Rouge survivors in Cambodia as well as abroad are the living proof.

I have looked into the eyes of the Khmer Rouge soldiers and even shared a home with them. When they later took Ai Sang Thout, I felt a knife in my heart that left a wound that doesn't heal. As a child, I saw adults unable to hide their fears, children my age left crying by the side of the road, and my parents face the challenge of tremendous uncertainty. The Khmer Rouge took something from all of its survivors, including me. For many Cambodians, like my mother, an irreplaceable part of their soul is gone, and their losses seem endless.

Had the war not occurred, chances are my life would have taken a very different path, Ai Sang Thout most likely would still be with our family, and an inconceivable 1.7 million people would not have met their death. Growing up I used to wish that I hadn't experienced the Khmer Rouge, but I can't change the past. It is what it is, as the saying goes. I've come to see that it's unfair to make myself suffer by dwelling on the evil things that occurred.

Now when I think of the Khmer Rouge, I no longer feel hatred and want revenge, but I still don't forgive them. Some people say you can't fully heal until you have forgiven those who hurt you. I disagree. I am content to withhold forgiveness and not be so hard on myself. The fact is, I miss Ai Sang Thout and continue to wonder about his life. Whether or not I ever learn the truth of what happened to him, I will cherish his memory.

Being a refugee has taught me that I can cope with and undertake any difficulty. These days when I'm in a tough situation, I remind myself that if I survived the Khmer Rouge and its effects on my family, I can survive anything.

I've told myself time and time again that writing this memoir was unavoidable. Perhaps I was even fated to do so. Through the process of writing it, I have learned a great deal: details of my parents background, how to deal with the war that took away Ai Sang Thout and so many Cambodians, how to overcome the feeing of being part of the under-class, how to not feel ashamed of being a refugee who needs charity and government assistance, and why I struggled in my youth. In Nepal I discovered it wasn't so bad to be me after all. Similarly, by digging through my past, I have found some semblance of peace. The new additions to our family who were born in the States have very little knowledge about what happened. Through this book I hope they will learn about our failures and triumphs as well as our extraordinary journey of survival.

Now that I have come to maturity, I eagerly want to share my story. I am hopeful that those who have the chance to read *Shoulders to Freedom* may find this a small contribution to Cambodia history and the Nyaw history or perhaps, if their experience has been similar to mine, a confirmation that the journey from the past to the present is always worth understanding.

Made in the USA
Middletown, DE
30 April 2021